From Crack to Christ: A Witness

SERVANT WITNESS ENDURING A FIERY TRIAL

by

April Cofield-Lambert

Gotham Books
30 N Gould St.
Ste. 20820, Sheridan, WY 82801
https://gothambooksinc.com/

Phone: 1 (307) 464-7800

© 2024 *April Cofield-Lambert*. All rights reserved.

No part of this book may be reproduced, stored in a retrieval system, or transmitted by any means without the written permission of the author.

Published by Gotham Books (December 11, 2024)

ISBN: 979-8-3305-8396-6 (H)
ISBN: 979-8-3305-8391-1 (P)
ISBN: 979-8-3305-8392-8 (E)

Because of the dynamic nature of the Internet, any web addresses or links contained in this book may have changed since publication and may no longer be valid.

The views expressed in this work are solely those of the author and do not necessarily reflect the views of the publisher, and the publisher hereby disclaims any responsibility for them.

Contents

Acknowledgements ix
Introduction x
Servant Witness Enduring a Fiery Trial 1
The Crack Head's Baby 8
A Big Girl 13
My First Job 19
Girl with a Baby 24
My First Bid 27
A Young Mother Makes A Choice 33
Ka'wand's Placement 36
Deep 40
Part of a Deal 42
Terrace Ave 46
My First Day on Terrace 47
Terrace Ave: The Beginning 54
My New Friend: Crack 55
Prostitute Paradise 59
Muscle Memory 62
No Place for Kids 64
Jailing 68
The Bearer of the Torch 73
Commissary 75
News of My Son 76
The Stroll 80
A Woman's Worth 83
Occupational Hazards 85

The Right Choice.. 88
The Commandeer.. 89
The Beam Team 91
The Ones that Prayed for me 94
Encounter with Infamous Serial Killer 96
My Nose Ring 98
Short Stays.. 104
Decline... 107
I Want You 108
The Death of April Cofield February 16, 1995................... 109
Rebirth of the Spiritual Woman 112
No Testimony Without a Test 115
TOPIC House 121
My First Day.. 123
A Woman's Smile... 126
High Risk Category... 128
More Memories of TOPIC House.. 132
Six dollars and a Dream 138
Good News in The Mail 140
The Call.. 141
The Deployment... 143
The church with the big steps 144
Boldness Meets Humility 145
A Passed Torch... 147
Learning to Trust 150
A Promise Kept... 157
A Prayer Answered 163
Afterword 164
The "Life Puzzel" That Came Together.............................. 165

This book is dedicated to the following people:

This book is dedicated to the following people:

To My Boaz, Deacon Kevin Lambert, whose unwavering faith and support have been my cornerstone.

To my son, Ka'wand Cofield, and my daughter, Don'yat Graham, who are my joy and blessing.

To my precious grandchildren, Don'tay Colin Graham and Princess Cofield, who fill my life with boundless love and joy.

To the Terrace Avenue Survivors, whose courage and perseverance are a testament to the power of hope.

To Rev. Reginald Tuggle and Memorial Presbyterian Church, for their spiritual guidance and unwavering faith.

To my Sunday School Teacher, Ms. B, for her wisdom and patience.

To the Cofield and Lambert families, for their unending support and love.

And always to THE LOST, THE LEAST, AND THE LAST.

Minister April Cofield-Lambert

For Don'tay, Princess and Jaslynn.
In Loving Memory of My Madear, Lee Branch
My Dad, Bobby Cofield, My Niece Tameka Williams,
Mother-in-law Barbra Jean Lambert,
and Mrs. Inez Graham.

Don't let your <u>location</u> or your <u>situation</u> be the basis of your <u>identification</u> or you will place a <u>limitation</u> on your ultimate <u>destination</u>. The Preacher.

When reading this marvelous book one is immediately struck with three conflicting emotions. First, there is the overwhelming notion of one's own grace. Except by the grace of God this story could be about me.

Second, a mystery is revealed that only by reading the book can one discover the answer. The mystery is surrounded by the questions, "How does a person locked into such a complex and self-degrading situation get out of that mess?" The person has little education, almost no family support system, no spiritual circle of friends, no money, no sense of spiritual self-awareness, and no prospects of ever moving from where she is to another and higher level of existence. The reader will see episodes in his/her own life that seemed hopeless and yet somehow someway one survived and moved on to higher and better places. This is what makes life so exciting; we never know how God will deliver us from a situation and yet, if we allow it, He rescues us each and every time. This is what the world or non-believer doesn't understand. This is also why we remain faithful, because God is faithful unconditionally.

Third, profound joy and a sense of the indomitability of the human spirit will burn in your soul as you see how a new identity and a fresh sense of self-awareness propelled this woman to be a blessing to so many to others. She didn't leave a hellish existence never to return. She left to embrace her savior, Jesus Christ, and then returned to rescue others by bringing them the GOOD NEWS. She went back to an old situation, in the same location, but with a different identification. Now, buried within her bosom is the Love of Jesus Christ for others. As April says, "There is no testimony without a test." So tirelessly, even though she continues to fight demons, she preservers, determined to fight in the name of Jesus Christ the arch enemy of heaven, the Devil himself so that her life will make a difference in God's Kingdom. It matters for her son and daughter especially, and for those still locked in hell's grip.

The writer of the book, Robin Marshall, led by the Holy Spirit, captured in a few words the life, death, and rebirth of a woman who was once lost and now is found. On behalf of the thousands whose lives will be blessed by having read this book, I say to Robin, THANK YOU. May God continue to rest His blessings on you, your ministry, and your family.

Rev. Reginald Tuggle, Sr. Pastor
Memorial Presbyterian Church
Roosevelt, New York

Acknowledgements

I must acknowledge and thank my Lord and Savior Jesus Christ, without Him in my life, I would be nothing. I want to thank those who have been praying for me, standing in the gap with me, my family, Ka'wand, Don'yat and Don'tay, Madear and my sisters and brothers, my dear friend, Robin and her family, "Not- So-Secret", my "Sister Girl", my armor bearers, my colleagues, my God daughter Nessa, Rev. Tuggle, Rev. Crayton and Pastor "Vonnie", MPC Prison Ministry, my Brothers and Sisters on the Inside, my Mentees on the Outside, the Correction Officers, Choresis Dance Ministry, and my church family.

April

Thank you, Lord, for calling me by name. Honor and thanks to my husband and family for their unyielding support. To my prayer partners and support team. To my daughter and my niece for reading countless pages over and over again. Love you all so much. We couldn't have done this without your support.

Robin

Introduction

Servant Witness, Enduring a Fiery Trial

I am profoundly grateful for the journey that has brought me here. My path has been fraught with challenges and trials, but it has also been brightened. by the grace of God. I am a testament to the truth that only God can judge me. People, including Christians and believers, have often scorned and ridiculed me. But then I remember that my Lord and Savior, Jesus Christ, endured the same.

Throughout my life, I have been called many names:

- Evangelist
- Minister
- Rev. April
- Author
- Sister April
- Ms. April

And even less flattering ones:

- Mean
- Bitch
- Crackhead
- Prostitute

But please allow me to reintroduce myself: I am a servant and child of the Most High God, in Jesus Christ's name. My name just happens to be April.

It has been 16 years since the release of "From Crack to Christ: A Witness," and now, by the grace and mercy of God, I celebrate 30 years clean and sober. I am an ordained and licensed Minister of the gospel of Jesus Christ. I have experienced the pain of divorce and the joy of remarriage. I have welcomed another granddaughter into my life. I have endured the sorrow of losing both my parents and the devastating discovery of my niece's death. I have been working in a place for 25 years where they said I had no business being. I am the living founder of the Terrace Avenue Survivors Reunion.

This introduction marks a new chapter in my journey. After the release of "From Crack to Christ: A Witness," I continue to stand firm no matter what! as a Witness to the power of God's Grace, Mercy, and Love. In Jesus Christ's name, Amen.

This is a story about April. She and I attend Memorial Presbyterian Church in Roosevelt, NY. She is an attractive, thick woman with a nose ring and beautifully manicured nails. She sits on the right side of the church. Second row. Aisle seat. She religiously sends up a prayer card, asking for prayers for the prison ministry and the laborers that go in with her every third Sunday. She would also include a request for prayers for two family members who were both incarcerated at the time. I never really knew much about her but I was intrigued and watched her from a distance.

I sat in the back row. Sometimes the right side, but mostly on the left. The last three rows in our church are reserved for families with small children. Who ever thought of that idea was a genius. There is a general tendency to feel at ease when you are in the company of other families who also have noisy children. My children are older now, and it is only through grace and mercy that the ushers still let me sit in that section. From this viewing area, I can see the pulpit, the choir loft and most of the parishioners. That is how I saw April.

April was then and still is to this day very vocal in her worship. Just like the disciples who loudly shouted out their adoring words of worship to Jesus. The bible says that: Some of the Pharisees from among the multitude said unto him, Master, rebuke thy disciples. And He answered and said unto them, "I tell you that, if these should hold their peace, the stones would immediately cry out." (Luke 19:39-40 KJV). April tells the stones, "I got this!" as she praises God loudly every Sunday without fail. Shedding cleansing tears of joy and thanksgiving. Praising Him and thanking Him loudly with arms elongated and hands out-stretched towards Heaven.

I love watching April worship God this way. Her form of praise reminds me of the women in the church of my youth. I attended a Baptist Church in Farmville, NC. The women and men prayed. praised and worshipped God until they were physically exhausted. That was April. Some of the parishioners preferred she sit down, but she would not. If only they knew. If only they knew the hell she'd been through, they would've joined her in this glorious praise and worship to her God who delivered her from the pit of hell.

In the fall of 2000, I enrolled as an adult student at the local community college. I was very nervous on my first day of classes and was unable to find my way around the campus. I went to the information desk and lo and behold, there was April. I didn't know that she was an employee there. She helped me find my way to class and afterwards offered additional assistance if I needed it. With time, I soon learned my way around campus but, it was comforting knowing that she was there just in case. We started chatting regularly, still within the confines of the normal niceties that people exchange. But that was about to change.

One morning, I parked my car in the main parking lot near the Tower. I didn't usually park on that side of campus. I preferred to park near the campus childcare facility. My one-year-old son attended the program there while I attended classes. But that particular morning, the parking lot near the childcare facility was full so I parked near the Tower. I hated parking near the Tower! There were so many accidents in that parking area and the students would follow you to your car to get your parking space. I didn't blame them. Parking spaces were limited, but what if I wanted to go to my car to get a nap between classes? What if I just wanted to go to my car and let it warm up before driving off? I always felt pressured into leaving immediately. On this day I was followed by yet another student so without waiting to warm up the car, begrudgingly, I pulled out of the lot. And there at the bus stop was April. I pulled over in front of her and rolled down the passenger side window,

"Get in."

"But you're not going my way."

"I am now!"

I moved my jacket and backpack off the seat and she got in.

"Where's the baby?"

"He stayed at home, today. How are you?"

We continued with minor chit chat. And then she started to share her story. I should probably stop and tell you that it is not uncommon for this to happen. I've grown accustomed to perfect strangers coming up to me in public places and freely telling me their life story. They say that I am a great listener. But if you ask my children who painstakingly try to convince me to change my mind once I've said "no", they may beg to differ. But back to April. I didn't know much about her personal life; I only knew that she had been incarcerated. She started telling me the story of a young mother, a prostitute, a crack addict and a woman who was destined to spend the better part of seventeen years in jail. Wow! I knew we would have general conversation en route to her apartment, but not once did I expect to hear this on our ten-minute ride. The ten minutes turned into thirty-five. And it was on this ride, our first of many, that she told me the following story, one that I would never forget.

Servant Witness
Enduring a Fiery Trial

To Whom Much is given much is required. Luke 12:48

Really Lord Jesus, really? What is this about? As I ponder over the various seasons of my life, I find myself reflecting on all the trials and tribulations that only God could see me through. I'm weeping, I'm crying I even feel like screaming, WHY ME? WHY ME LORD JESUS? thank God for a deep personal relationship with the Most High, WHY NOT YOU. The Lord God reminded me of all that I asked of Him.

I'LL GO LORD! SEND ME LORD! One thing for sure is that the saying is indeed true be careful of what you pray for especially the will of God to be done. It was amazing the reactions from people about the telling of my life story, some indicated they could not put it down others stated that I understand you better now that I have read your book? It's 15 years later and 30 years clean and sober. Before I go on. Allow me to define Servant Witness.

<u>**Servant Witness**</u> A servant focuses on doing his or her master's will. And a Witness testifies to what he or she has seen and personally experienced. As a redeemed daughter and child of God, I am called to both. According to Acts 26:16 The Bible calls folks to be both witnesses and servants to God. From Crack to Christ A: Witness, really took off, speaking to various organizations, parolees, probation officers, domestic violence survivors, families of addicted family members giving insights on how to get a job with multiple felonies.

Hearing and seeing the identification of those who knew exactly what I had been through, discovering the realness of generational curses.

Shopping in the super market and feeling like I'm being followed, only to discover I was by people who had read From Crack to Christ A

Witness. Listening to what they were feeling, praying with them, crying with them, at times only to utter JESUS, PLEASE HELP ME TO HELP THEM! Still going in to the jail, still sharing my experience, strength and hope. Still going into a place that housed me from 1978-1989 off and on in and out, My God, My God.

Fiery Trial 1 Peter 4:12-19 New King James Version

Suffering for God's Glory

[12] Beloved, do not think it strange concerning the fiery trial which is to try you, as though some strange thing happened to you; [13] but rejoice to the extent that you partake of Christ's sufferings, that when His glory is revealed, you may also be glad with exceeding joy. [14] If you are [a]reproached for the name of Christ, blessed *are you,* for the Spirit of glory and of God rests upon you. [b]On their part He is blasphemed, but on your part He is glorified. [15] But let none of you suffer as a murderer, a thief, an evildoer, or as a [c]busybody in other people's matters. [16] Yet if *anyone suffers* as a Christian, let him not be ashamed, but let him glorify God in this [d]matter.

[17] For the time *has come* for judgment to begin at the house of God; and if *it begins* with us first, what will *be* the end of those who do not obey the gospel of God? [18] Now

"If the righteous one is scarcely saved,
Where will the ungodly and the sinner appear?"

[19] Therefore let those who suffer according to the will of God commit their souls *to Him* in doing good, as to a faithful Creator.

Thus say the Lord God. Why did I find it strange that God would raise me up? Why did I find it strange that the My God would do what He promised He would do? In all of that God did not allow me to have a give up nor a given in spirit. Of course, I felt like giving up and giving in, of course I wanted to mis represent My Lord and Savior Jesus the Christ, of course I wanted to fly a few heads, yes, I said it. God taught me to Stand Firm No Matter What. God said trust me April.

Now I'm speaking in places that would never have had me in their churches, colleges, spaces or places, I'm smiling as I write this cause folks just didn't want to believe that God would do it for a wretch like me. That in telling my story God will get all the glory, honor and praise. I found it amazing how we tend to put God in a box, realizing He's too big, He's to mighty and powerful. From Crack to Christ: A Witness opened and closed doors for me. Having people approach me about their concerns for my son and daughter was especially challenging.

Enduring a fiery trial made me realize that God would not have brought me this far to let me go. And to always prepare myself to give an answer to the why Jesus Christ is so real to me. Every time I'm asked that question, I think about my head would have been chopped off if had not been for the Lord Jesus Christ, (pause) what do you mean what do I mean? I cried out Lord Jesus Help Me and that man, that person who was going to kill me seen my Nose ring, in the dark, in the woods, in the heat of his anger to get revenge on the person who destroyed his life and he thought that person was me.

Of course, there are many that would like the in-depth detail of the writings of From Crack to Christ: A Witness I'm smiling because you have to see The Lord Jesus about that.

Even book me for an event/book discussion/speaking engagement I'm still smiling.

The Prayer's and Scriptures, God gave me to Pray

This Pray is called the 4H prayer.

Lord Jesus Christ Please

Help Me, Humble Me, Heal Me, and Hide Me, behind your cross don't let them see me, let them see You, Lord Jesus Christ, so that Thy and Only thy will get the Glory, Honor and Praise.

Psalm 141:3 lord Help Me control my tongue, help me be careful about what I say (NCV) ~ In Jesus Christ name Amen

Psalm 121~ All of my Help comes from the Lord

Lord Jesus Christ, I love you and I need you I'm nothing without You.

The Songs God Gave me to praise Him.

When I think about the Lord, how He saved me, how He raised me how He healed me to the utter the most, When I think about the Lord, how He picked me up and turned me around and place my feet on solid ground it makes me want to shout hallelujah, thank you Jesus Lord Your worthy of all the glory, all the honor and all the praise.

As I conclude this part, I would like to mention the husband God sent to me, My Boaz, Deacon Kevin Lambert, A man God knew was for me. Kind mild mannered, tolerant, compassionate, I only asked God for a man that loves Him. Realizing that if that man loved God he would love me.

The Terrace Avenue Survivors Reunions brought a lot of joy to my heart to pray on the block that would have killed me and so many others had it not been for God. Praying in the middle section of 100 Terrace Avenue, wearing our purple and white, touching and agreeing, in the spirit of the living God in Jesus Christ name, inviting others to stand in the gap with me, and for me, was simply amazing and indeed only God.

The Lost, The Least, and The Last~ That's where I come from

Bloodlines: A Cofield Legacy~ I come from a very unique bloodline.

Terrace Avenue Survivors~ We Are Terrace Avenue

As the revising and upgrading of my book continues, it is always my prayer that God would always give me the prayers to pray and the words to say. Yes, it's my story yet...I'm giving My Abba Father God All the Glory, Honor and Praise in Jesus Christ name Amen.

We Might Have Done What The devil Said We Did,

But We are Not who the devil Says We Are.

I am a servant and child of the Most high God in Jesus Christ, my name just happens to be

April Cofield Lambert~ Minister/Evangelist

Grace and Peace Dearest Heart's.

Stand Firm No Matter What.

Can a woman forget her sucking child, that she should not have compassion on the son of her womb? Yea, they may forget, yet will I not forget thee.
(Isaiah 49:15KJV)

The Crack Head's Baby

People that smoke crack are creatures of habit like other people. For example: most people that drink coffee must have a cup first thing in the morning. They will put on that coffee pot before washing up. If they don't have it at home, they'll leave for work early enough to drive by 7-Eleven to get a cup of coffee. I was no different. I once lived on the second floor right above a crack den. It was very convenient, so, whenever I wanted a hit, I would just walk down stairs. This particular morning was no different than any other and I needed my first hit of the day. I no longer lived on the second floor but, I knew that I could get in the apartment with no problem. So I walked to the door, turned the doorknob, and let myself in. When I got in, there were crack heads everywhere. They were laying on the couch. On the floor. I was amazed that there were so many people crammed in that small one-bedroom apartment. Over in one corner, there were a couple of people piled up on top of each other. Legs were spread everywhere and I couldn't tell whose legs belonged to who. It was cool outside but it was stuffy in the front room and it smelled like a combination of clothes that were stale from being soaked in sweat, urine, and dried up s---! I wanted to hold my breath, handle my business and quickly get out of there. I was in a hurry. Had to hit the streets. And so, I stepped over them to get to the lady who rented the apartment who was also the dealer. She was in a corner with a crack pipe in her hand. Looking a mess! Her hair was smashed down on one side like she slept on it. The other side wasn't any better. It wasn't smashed down but it had lint in it. A comb wouldn't have done her hair much good. She needed some scissors. I'd seen stray dogs on the street whose matted fur looked better than hers. She had white crust around her mouth and when she opened her lips, there was a slimy film at the part where the skin meets. But when you're smoking, you don't care about that. There's only one thing you care about: chasing that high!

I was moving closer to her, when all of a sudden, I heard crying that was coming from the backroom. I waited, but no one seemed to be getting up to check it out. So stepping over more stretched out bodies, I opened the door to the back bedroom. Then it hit me. Hard! I got a whiff of a smell that was stronger than the one in the front room. It smelled really pissy. There in the corner was this baby on a pissy-smelling, urine-soaked mattress. That baby had been sitting in that urine for so long that his plastic diaper had blown up and was falling apart. The material inside the diaper had come apart and was beaded up on his thighs and little pieces of wet paper and plastic were on his stomach. The baby was so wet that the diaper had leaked and there were wet stains on the mattress. The mattress was not in a frame so; the floor beneath the mattress had changed colors. There were other brown spots on the mattress, too. This wasn't the first time it had happened but this time, the baby had been possibly sitting for days.

I looked back out into the living room at his mom. She was so high. She was locked with no combination. I knew exactly where she was, and there is no room for babies in that place. I turned back around and looked even closer at the baby. The baby was crying and scratching his arms and his neck. He had a flaky rash that was itching him. It looked familiar. My own son, Ka'Wand had eczema and used to scratch like that when he was a baby. My children were no longer with me so seeing this baby took me back to the times when my own baby suffered all night. Itching and scratching sometimes until his skin became raw and would bleed. Damn! This could easily be my son.

I had enough money to buy two rocks. I thought for a minute. I needed to make the baby feel better. I turned and left the room, stepped back over bodies and left the crack den to go to the store around the corner. I went outside and I'm walking fast and praying all the way there, "Lord, please don't let a trick pull up before I get to this store and get back."

"Why were you praying about that?"

"If a trick had pulled up, I would've gotten in that car. That's my money. It's all about the loot, Baby!"

I was silent. She continued.

"I made it to the store. I bought a loaf of bread, some mayonnaise and meat and a bottle of crack head juice."

I stopped her.

"What's crack head juice?"

"It's that juice that you get from the deli in the little plastic jug that cost about twenty-five cents. You know the one." I did.

"But why do you call it crack head juice?"

"Because it doesn't cost a lot. That juice and a Little Debbie is crack food. It gives you just enough to get the edge off without using up your crack money."

I also bought diapers and picked up a newspaper. I went back. I laid the newspaper down on the mattress and changed the baby. I made the baby a sandwich and gave him the juice. I held him as I had once held my own son when he suffered. I rubbed his skin in the places where he had been scratching. I knew it itched really bad. It even looked like it hurt. He put his head on my chest I rubbed his little arms and his back while rocking him back and forth. Soon, he fell asleep in my arms. I laid him down on another place of the mattress that was dry. I took off my jacket and folded it. I placed it down underneath the baby's head. As I was leaving, I told the mother to give the rest of the food to the baby later or tomorrow. I bought my crack and then I left.

April stopped talking. She couldn't say any more about it. I looked at her. She looked at me. We sat in silence. So many thoughts were running through my head. I thought about all the times I've purchased those jug juices for my children and also I'm thinking that I'm looking at a reformed crack head ho with a conscience! I looked at her and she at me. Then tears started to flow down her face. I felt badly for thinking what I did. I reached over and intertwined my fingers with hers and held her hand until she stopped crying. As we continued to sit with the silence broken only by the muffled sounds of stifled cries, images are running through my mind. The first: the quiet comfort of a baby who sleeps on a pissy-smelling mattress in a crack den. Second: the jug juices, colored with red and blue dyes that stain your tongue, your teeth, and the rim above your upper lip. The same jug juices that my own children have enjoyed on warm summer afternoons. And another thought, after today, I will not purchase another one.

That evening as I arrived in my driveway, I was amazed that I made it there alive. The car must've been on autopilot, I swear, because I don't remember seeing the lights, traffic or anything else. All I could think of was the story. Her story. And then all of these thoughts begin flooding my mind. How could this happen? What kind of person could get involved in the lifestyle that she described? Not the April I've seen in church. The one that praises God with tears and vocal utterances of thanksgiving! Not her. As I said previously, I had grown accustom to people sharing their life stories with me and my being able to let it go. This time it was different. I couldn't let it go. I wanted to know what happened. I wanted to know her truth. I needed to know her testimony.

In time, over eight years, I'd get answers to all of my questions. I didn't know how deep I'd have to go in to get those answers. I've come to realize that it was deeper than I ever imagined possible. The most difficult task on this project was not what I learned about her but, what I learned about myself. Hearing her truth, forced me to face my own.

So, chosen for His purpose, as she has told it to me, I'll in turn, tell it to you. And then you'll understand why she praises with unadulterated thanksgiving! From Crack to Christ: A Witness? Yes, indeed. You'll see. Yes, indeed.

Children, obey your parents in all things:
for this is well- pleasing unto the Lord.
(Colossians 3:20KJV)

A Big Girl

"April, be a big girl. Be a good girl.
And remember to pray."

That simple request of my mother has always framed who I am and who I would become. I always tried to do what my mother wanted me to do. I was a big girl. Check! That request was taken care of. I was big boned, large for my age. Still am. I've always been thick. Next request? I tried to be a good girl. Check! I really did. Double check! And remembering to pray? Believe me. I prayed and I prayed. And when I didn't, I know that there were others who prayed for me. I know there are many mothers who have made this same request of their children. Mothers that are there when you need them, no matter what. Mothers that will give you their last and go without. I always tried to do what my Madear wanted me to do. That's what I called my mother, Madear. All I ever really wanted was to be near her. Ironically, I still do. I love my Madear and I'm sure she loves me. All children think that. Don't they?

My mother met my father at a bar in Hempstead, NY. She was the tender age of fifteen but she looked much older because, she was very shapely. She lived in Jamaica, NY, with her stepmother and her cousin because she was abandoned by her birth mother when she was young.

My mother and her cousin enjoyed going out. They felt grown up as they sat in the bars, laughing, dancing, and having a good time. One evening, my father laid eyes on her and knew right away that he had to meet her. Her cousin noticed the handsome dark complexioned man looking at her and introduced him to my mother. As the story goes, he liked her right away and asked for her phone number. She gave it to him. He called the next day and asked her stepmother if he could take my mother to the movies. And the rest, they say, is history.

My earliest childhood memories have always been with me and my sisters. After I was born, every year thereafter, Madear was having a baby. Me in 1961, one in 1962, one in 1963, and one in 1964. Madear was nineteen with four children. My father was twenty-two. A good-looking man. He was a mechanic by trade. I fondly remember that he always had black oil on his clothes and on his hands. He was always greasy from working on cars. We lived together on Seaman Ave. in Freeport, NY.

My parents had their ups and downs like most couples. Sometimes they would argue and my aunt would come, get us and take us to her house. She didn't want us to hear the heated arguments and the name calling. After a while, they would make up and my aunt would take us back home. My parents would be happy for a little while and then my father would go back out there and mess around. He was a womanizer. That's what most of the arguments were about. He was out there ripping and running the streets. Sleeping with this one and that one. Women would call the house and talk about my father to Madear. It hurt her so bad. She was tired of being confronted by all these other women who were telling her about him and what they had done together. She grew weary and just couldn't take it any longer. So, like her mother left her, she left us.

I can't remember much from my childhood, but I do remember the day that my life turned upside down. I woke up and Madear was putting away groceries. I could tell even as a young girl that there was something wrong. Something different about the way she emptied the bags. She was moving so quickly. Going from one bag to another and then another. There were grocery bags everywhere. She'd gotten up early and gone shopping and the refrigerator was stocked full. Milk and bread. Cereal. Eggs. You name it. All the food that we liked to eat was in the house. I was standing there looking around and watching her and then she saw me. She came over to me and said this:

"April, be a big girl. Be a good girl. And remember to pray." I always tried to do what my mother wanted me to do.

"Okay, Madear, I will."

I thought she was just going out for a while but then, I saw her suitcases and other bags. I knew she was going somewhere but, I didn't see my stuff packed. Our stuff packed.

"Can I go, Madear?"

She didn't answer me. She told me again to be a good girl. And with that she grabbed her suitcases, her other bags, and walked

out.

My father worked during the day, so he wasn't able to take care of us like Madear did. He asked my aunt, his sister, to come live with us and take care of us. She was a disciplinarian. Very strict. She would comb our hair at night and put a scarf on it so she wouldn't have to comb it in the morning. If it was messed up that next morning, she'd hit our hands.

I missed my mother. Especially at night. No bedtime stories or watching TV could calm me down for sleep. The only thing that worked was twirling my hair. I would carefully slide a braid out from underneath the scarf and then wrap it around my pointer finger. I would twirl it over and over again. I'd try to fix it in the morning. "April Marie!" my aunt called me. "Have you been messing with your hair?" She knew the answer already, as strands around the edges were pulled out of the neatly plaited braids. Some of the braids were unraveled from the roots. I would extend my hands to her and wait for the stinging pain from the hairbrush. Sometimes, I'd pull my hands back and the brush would get my knuckles instead of the fleshy part of the palm of my hands. I used to try my best to fix my hair before she could see it, but I was only four years old.

Sometimes on Sunday afternoons, my father would take us on a long drive to the big house. We'd drive there, sometimes in complete silence. It must've been a boarding house for ladies. The big house; that's what I called it. My Madear lived there. She would come out, talk to us, and hug us. "Be a big girl, be a good girl! And don't forget to pray." I use to look forward to the long drives to the big house. I missed Madear. My father wasn't an affectionate man. This lack of affection only made me miss her more. I've tried to remember but, I can't ever remember him telling me he loved me.

After some time, Madear left the big house and she wanted custody of us. We had to go to family court. My first of many courthouse appearances. The wood on the bench where we sat was shiny and smooth. It was cold at first but, got warmer as you sat on it. We sat there while the grownups talked about what was best for us. I could see my father pacing around in circles. He stopped to listen to the judge. It was decided that we would live with my mother. He sat down and then he looked over at us. He may have never told me he loved me, but that day, the look on his face told me that he did.

We moved that same week to Maplewood Dr. Westbury, NY. Madear was so happy to be with us. We had a nice place to live. Madear took us shopping and bought us the most beautiful clothes. She would dress all of us in matching outfits. The Cofield girls always looked nice. We also had nice bikes. This was back in the day when a new bike meant a lot on the block. It was a status symbol. Me, my sisters, and my friend across the street spent a lot of time in our backyard, which was near a hill that leads down to the Wantagh Parkway. We use to lie on our stomachs and roll down the hill. It's a miracle that one of us didn't end up rolling onto the parkway. It was so much fun. If we weren't at home, we were across the street at my friend's home. We had some really good times on Maplewood, and then things started to go bad.

Madear started going out, getting high and using dope. To support her habit, she started prostituting. Sometimes in our home, and most of the time when she went out. She was a good looking, shapely woman and those country boys in Westbury loved her. There were many male visitors in our home to see my Madear. She began using all of the rent money for her dope habit. Soon after, we were evicted from Maplewood Dr. and with nowhere to go, we moved to The Cottage Hotel* in Great Neck. The Cottage Hotel was used for emergency housing and for low-income families. We attended the local school. And we called the hotel home for a few years.

April and I decided that we would meet on Fridays to prepare for the book. I would tape record the sessions or take notes.

On one Friday outing, April and I started talking about teenagers and jobs. Talking with her reminded me that a first job is often a source of pride. It is when a child no longer has to hold out a hand to a parent for candy money. Or when a teenager no longer needs to ask for cash to go to the mall, hang out with friends, or purchase that latest outfit. That first job is also when we learn the value of a dollar. There is a general tendency to spend your money more wisely when you've had to break a sweat or sacrifice and put in hours at a low paying job when you'd rather hang out with your friends.

My oldest two children and my niece have had the experience of making their own money. It's amusing to see how frugal they become when I ask to borrow money to avoid going to the cash machine late at night. Or, heaven forbid, if I should ask for gas money for driving them to work, to the mall, or recreational events. How dare I ask them for a dime after they've slaved for eight or ten hours a week! Shouldn't I just take care of their needs? That's what parents are supposed to do right? Take care of their children's needs.

It was 1975, when I began working my first job. It would become an annual summer job. As the daughter of a sharecropper, I joined my brothers and sisters before me by working in the tobacco fields. It was liberating knowing that I'd receive one hundred dollars cash for working from six in the morning to three or four in the afternoon. My son is fifteen and can only work ten hours a week so, I'm certain that child labor laws were broken to get in that crop. The work was monotonous but thanks to my brothers, nephews and my cousin, we somehow managed to make those long hours fun! There were other children from the community that joined us in the field and in many fields across the Piedmont section of North Carolina. Some of the money earned was used to hang out with our friends, but the bulk of it went to purchase school clothes for the following year.

It was at this outing that I realized that April and I had the year 1975 in common. April also joined the workforce that same year. I was twelve years old. April was fourteen.

*The rod and reproof give wisdom: but a child left
to himself bringeth his mother to shame.
(Proverbs 29:15KJV)*

My First Job

Things were gradually getting worse. Madear didn't know that everything she did affected us. Everything. Her drama became our drama. When things got really bad, my father would come and get us. Things would be normal for a while. My stepmother had even started reaching me about my hygiene. How to take care of my body. I could sit back and be a child when I was with them. Madear would get it together for a little while and we'd go back to live with her. Back and forth. Back and forth. I felt like a child in one world and an adult in another.

Madear started jostling, boosting and short-conning. By now, I was a young teen and growing up fast. We had been exposed to a lot of things. Madear didn't have to tell us to be big girls or good girls anymore. We were big. At least I was. I was shaped just like my mother. We'd learned to take care of ourselves. One of my sisters used to ride the bike to the grocery store and bring back cigarettes and meat. I had started running away, cutting classes, smoking a little weed and drinking golden champale. Madear never told us that our behavior was wrong. She just told us don't get caught.

By now, I'm fourteen and we were back in Freeport. Things were really bad now and the mood of the house was based on how Madear felt that day. Madear was either high on heroin or from snorting cocaine. Our basic necessities had run out. There was no food in the house.

"Madear, I'm hungry."

I started looking in every cabinet to see if I could find something, but the cabinets were bare. She finally spoke and what she said was about to change the course of my life.

"I can't feed you! I can't even take care of you! So get out!"

Out of all the stuff that we'd been through, she had never told me to leave. She would leave us, but she never told one of us to leave. I sat there trying to process what I was hearing. It didn't add up. It just didn't. Anyway, I didn't have anywhere to go. No one wanted to be bothered with me because of my behavior.

"What should I do, Madear?"

I was so afraid. And I was angry! It felt like I had that big lump in my throat that you sometimes get before you are about to cry. I waited for her answer. As I'm waiting, all these thoughts are going through my head. Why me? What did I do?! I knew how to be a good girl when I wanted to. I was already acting like a big girl. Had been doing that since she told me to be good when I was four. I waited. She didn't say a word. Sometimes silence is louder than spoken words. I knew what to do. I'd seen her do things that a daughter should never have to see her mother do. She'd taught me well. I just wanted her permission.

"Madear, please! I'm not hungry anymore!"

She said nothing. The lump in my throat dropped down into my stomach. I left the house crying. As I walked out the front door and down the steps to turn onto the sidewalk, my eyes had filled up with water. Then the tears came rushing down my face. "Why me? Why me? Why didn't the others have to leave? I didn't ask to come here!" I walked to the corner and turned. Didn't exactly know where I was going. I felt like I was all alone in the world. I felt like I couldn't even go to my father's family, the Cofields. I just knew that I was leaving my family and my home.

I was cold. Very, very cold. And I was still walking. Soon I heard this noise. I realized it was my stomach growling. I realized that I had lied to Madear, because I was still hungry. I stopped walking when I came to a bench on Main St. in Freeport. Didn't know that I was sitting on the stroll. I didn't know that the bench I'd chosen to sit on was used by people waiting for the bus by day and people available for drive thru service at night. Men would pull up in cars and the women and a few men would take their orders and get in and deliver it quickly. Get out and wait for the next customer. I sat on the bench crying. I was tired and lonely and I missed my sisters. I just wanted to be with them. Little did I know that it would soon be my turn to serve a customer. I had my head down. I'm trying not to stare at the activity going on around me but, I couldn't help it. Still crying, still cold and still hungry. I sat there for what seemed like hours but, it probably wasn't that long. After a while, it felt like somebody was staring at me. I looked up and there was this older white man in his car looking at me.

I stopped her.

"Do you remember his name?"

She gives me this look then answers sarcastically. "Yeah. Trick!"

She continues her story.

"You cold?", he asked me.

"Yes."

"You hungry?"

"Yes."

"Come sit in the car with me. I'll give you a warm jacket and something to eat. That'll make you feel better." By then it was very late and my head was aching from crying. I got in his car. He had the heat on. It was warm inside the car. He wrapped this blue jacket around my shoulders."

I stopped her again.

"Were you afraid to be getting in the car with a stranger? Hadn't anybody in your family ever told you about strangers? You didn't know him."

"I wasn't afraid of him. I had seen too much to be afraid of anyone that looked like him." Anyhow, we then drove down Main Street and turned onto Merrick Ave. in Freeport. He pulled up in front of the Imperial Diner. We went in and sat down.

She's on a roll, but I must stop her and ask:

"You actually sat down in the diner and had dinner? An older white male with a young black girl?"

"You have to remember. I didn't look my age. I was thick. I've always been thick. So, I looked much older than fourteen. He was talking to the waiters and the manager like he knew them or something. Evidently, it wasn't his first time going there with different women."

"Evidently. Do you remember what you ate that night?"

"No. I just remember sitting in the booth and there were people all around. And I'm sitting across the table from an older man. A man who I wasn't afraid of. A man who was showing me some kindness."

Well, after a while, we left the diner. We drove up to Sunrise Highway to a motel. He got the room. We went in and he started talking to me in a gentle manner. He told me what I needed to know like, what he liked, what made him feel good and what to expect. Everything from there happened so quickly. I got undressed. I did all of those things that he asked, then he lay on top of me. There was pressure. You know how when the dentist tells you, there might be some pressure? Well, there was pressure and then warmth. And maybe two, three minutes later, he was done. He liked them young, so he could teach them, I guess. And

I was a good student. A good girl. Just like Madear said. Afterwards, he dropped me back at the same corner. The same bench. But I was no longer a little girl. Some things in my life were about to change. I had a full stomach, a warm, blue jacket and for the first time: A twenty, a ten and a five. Dead presidents in my hand. I interviewed and landed my first job!

Growing up, there were two terms used for pregnant teens. One: young mother or two: a girl with a baby. The young mother was one that had probably spent a lot of time babysitting her siblings or neighborhood kids. She was the one that the old folks said would make it because "She sho is good to dem kids!" A girl with a baby. on the other hand, probably spent a lot of time running around. She may have even been labeled a tomboy. What would she know about taking care of children?

I fell in the latter category. Only family would dare ask me to babysit. And those requests were few and far between. I was twenty- four and not married when I became pregnant with my daughter. Chronologically old enough but, there was strong speculation almost to the point of certainty that I'd be a girl with a baby. Putting my wants and needs ahead of the baby. Not wanting or taking the time to properly see to the needs of the child because, I would need my rest or even worse putting the child on the edge of the bed and walking out of the room! I must admit that I too, was concerned for the welfare of my baby. I read all of the books and prayed that the nesting instinct would kick in.

It was 1989. My husband cut the umbilical chord and the doctor placed her in my arms. It was then that I became a mother. For April, it was 1978 and she was young and alone when she became a girl with a baby.

Girl with a Baby

After that night, my attitude changed towards my mom. I didn't want to be out there selling my body but it gave me the advantage of not having to ask for anything. I still tried to go to school but when you're holding down a full time job at night, it's kinda hard to stay awake in school. Everybody's got their priorities and making loot became mine. I became very promiscuous. I often wondered if Madear knew or more importantly, if she cared. Well, pretty soon, I had to abandon school. It was then that I also started smoking weed and shoplifting. I got caught once and was arrested. My first of many arrests. I was released on my own recognizance. By now, I had left Madear's home, permanently. I rented rooms. So, I went and came as I pleased.

I learned how to separate "my business" from my personal life. And that's when I met this man. When he told me his name, I laughed. Bobby. How ironic. The same name as my father's. We started hanging out. He was very handsome. We had some good times together.

Well, about this same time, I met a woman named Deidra*. She was out there like me, but she was older and had a daughter. Even though we both came out at night, she was in the process of doing better. She had gotten a two bedroom apartment at 100 Terrace Ave. She became like a big sister to me. A mentor. I guess I reminded her of herself when she was younger. She took me under her wing and taught me some things. She told me that I could do better if I had clients. She turned me on to a few. I'd meet them in their offices or hotels. You know, I often wondered if she was getting a cut. If she was pimping me. But, pimping me ain't ever been easy. I'm not gonna lay on my back and give you a cut. Never! Anyway, she tried to help me find something legit. She helped me find a job as a live-in.

I started working for this lady, name Georgia* who had two children. I babysat her children in exchange for food, room and board and a few dollars. All was well. I had a place to stay. I worked for her during the day and at night for myself. Everything was going fine, until I got pregnant. I told Bobby that I was pregnant and he asked if I was gonna keep it. If I wasn't gonna keep it, I wouldn't have told him I was pregnant. I could tell by his response that he had no intentions of being involved in the baby's life. So now I'm sixteen, alone, and about to have a baby.

I had morning sickness like you wouldn't believe. I was so sick that I couldn't keep my secret. I had to leave Georgia's house because I couldn't work anymore. With no place to go, I went back to Madear's house. She took me in. It was 1978. Time passed and by now everybody knew that I was having a baby. I'll never forget. There was a heat wave that summer. It was so hot that Madear wet a sheet with cool water once and wrapped it around me to keep me cool.

One evening, my sisters decided to throw a party. They had a D.J. and they served drinks and snacks. They charged folks to come in. I was there but I started feeling uncomfortable so I left and walked to the store. I really wanted some chocolate ice cream. When I got to the store, I ran into a guy named Ka'wand, who was on his way to my house.

"What are you doing out here?"

"I wanted some ice cream, so I walked up here to get it."

"You don't need to be out here like this. Let me get us a cab."

"It's not far. I can walk it"

"No, let me get us a cab."

He did. We got out of the cab and walked from the street towards the house. As I turned the key in the door, warm water ran down my legs. My water had broken. I screamed for my sisters and my mother. I was in so much pain and I was so scared. Someone called an ambulance. It finally came and took me to the hospital. The party was still going on so I went to the hospital, alone.

As his screams announced his entrance into the world, April was thrust into adulthood. Since the age of fourteen when she started her first job and recently over the previous nine months, her childhood had been removed. She named her son, Ka'wand, after the guy who hailed the cab.

Her mother was only sixteen when she had her. Now, April was seventeen with a baby of her own. How can she take care of this new baby, when she can barely care for herself? She was a girl with a baby.

I counted his ten little fingers and ten little toes. Yeah! They were all there. The two of us were all alone and all I could do was thank God for him.

My First Bid

After Ka'wand was born, I wanted to do the right thing. I was getting a check from Social Services to help me take care of him. I wanted to stay home and take care of my baby, but I still had that strong urge to run the streets, too. You gotta remember that I was seventeen and that's what seventeen year-olds do. One night after hanging out, I came home and told my Madear that Ka'wand needed some pampers and milk.

"April, you were out all night and you didn't buy the baby no pampers or milk?"

She was right. And that was the last time she had to say that to me. Ever! I started back doing what I was good at. My sister and I had the responsibility of taking care of things at home. She stole food from grocery stores and I prostituted and used the money to buy pampers, milk, eggs, bacon, and whatever else we needed in the house. I also bought weed for us to smoke. I had a lot of responsibilities so I thought I was grown. Thought I was.

October 1978, I was out strolling and was waiting for the next Trick to pull up. These two men came up to me and asked me if I knew what a short con was. I said, "Yeah!" I don't know why to this very day that I let them talk me into running that game. I didn't need to do it. I could've just done him and he would've given me the money I wanted. Anyway, my next trick came along. I lured him to a location with the promise of sex.

When we got there, the two men jumped him, beat him up and took all his money. They also took his car and changed the license plate. We rode around in Rockville Centre. We split the money three ways and then I went home. A few days later, I was in the bed with the baby. My mother started calling me, "April, come down here!" It sounded really important. So I got up and went down there to see what was the matter. When I get downstairs, there were two detectives standing in the living room.

"April Cofield?"

"Yes"

"You're under arrest for ...."

I felt like I was in a dream. They lead me away in handcuffs. What about my baby? Who will take care of my baby? I'm only seventeen. Who will take care of me?

At my arraignment, I found out that the other two men had a previous criminal record and were looking at several years. I had a prior record but it was sealed because the offenses occurred when I was a minor. So they placed the blame on me. I was given the county bullet of one year, which came down to serving eight months at Nassau County Correctional Facility.

When I was admitted, I was given a blue dress, two sheets, a blanket, a pillow and pillowcase, a towel, a plastic coffee cup, a bar of soap, a toothbrush, toothpaste and a metal spoon. They escorted me to my cell. I went in and made my bed and put my things away. Then I sat there. I sat there and looked around my tiny space.

I thought about Ka'wand and I missed him. I wondered who was taking care of him. Who was feeding him. Probably Karen. I wonder if anybody will call me or if anybody will accept my call. I was overwhelmed and I wanted to cry, but not now. Later. Not until those lights went out and the sound of my moans could blend in with the other women on my tier. Those of us who would cry for our babies beneath the cloak of night. I waited. And I waited. Ten o'clock came and I heard what I'd been waiting for. "Lights out!" The officer yelled. Then I climbed in my neatly made up bed between the sheets, laid my head on the pillow and waited. I heard the first moan, then a second. Then there was sobbing, then soon after, I too, joined them.

The next morning we had to wake up for breakfast at seven o'clock. I grabbed my spoon and headed for the metal table outside my cell. The food was alright. I mean, it wasn't seasoned like our food at home but, it wasn't bad, either. No matter what you ate, you had to use that spoon. Later on as I did my bid, I realized how important it was to keep that spoon. One day a spoon went missing and they locked down the entire tier until they could find that spoon. I made sure I kept my spoon close after that.

Word spreads quickly around a jail. The inmates knew about me or better yet, they knew my father. My father never gave me much but, he gave me a valuable tool that I used on the street and in the jail. He gave me his name. There were those that wanted to step to me but, they didn't because I was Bobby Cofield's daughter. He had served some time and was known on the street. So, out of respect to him, nobody messed with me and when they tried, someone would say, "That's Bobby Cofield's daughter." And they would step away. They wouldn't mess with me. He didn't give me too much else, but I was thankful for the Cofield name.

I can't remember my first roommate. We call them cellies. After seventeen years, I can't remember one from the other. I do remember that it's an experience to have to pull up your dress over your behind. Pull down your underwear, if you had on any, sit on the toilet, and try to urinate or have a bowel movement with everybody on your tier knowing your business. There are officers walking around in plain sight. There are other inmates looking out from their cells. The only thing that separates you from them is the metal horizontal bars that kept me inside my cell. If you can see them, you know they can see you. Knowing your business. I'm usually very regular but, days went by and I couldn't go to the bathroom. My stomach was bloated, but I had no door to close or solid wall to hide me from being seen. The other women would just get up and go to the toilet. Didn't they have any pride? Weren't they ashamed? For days I watched them act as though they had privacy. One day I woke up and realized that if they've seen one, they've seen them all. I walked over to the toilet, pulled up my dress, straddled the toilet seat, sat down and become one with it. Without looking. Without caring. I voided until I was empty of everything!

That same toilet that I became friends with, soon became a tool for communication. In 1978, in the old jail, there were fifty female inmates in the whole facility. There were men housed in the tier above us. We use to pump the bowl. That's when you sit on a pillow over the toilet and move up and down. It drains the water from the toilet. The men above us would do the same thing and with no water in our bowl or the one above us, this would clear the pipes. We would stick our heads in the toilet and talk to the men. It was so much fun. I would do this by myself or sometimes with other females in my cell. Sometimes, we'd get caught. When we did, that meant a twenty-one day lock in. It was worth it though to hear a man's voice talk sweet to you. The only other men that talked to you were the officers and they were barking orders. So, yeah, it was worth it.

The best thing that happened to me during this bid was "The Church on the Inside." It was also the only time since I was a little girl that I went to church. It soon became my church home. The Church on the Inside was held in the laundry room. There were folding chairs set up and only six people attended the services. The service lasted about forty five minutes. I can't remember what her first sermon was. I just remember feeling the presence of God. And for that brief forty five minutes, in the laundry room with five other inmates and the pastor, I could listen to the word of God and be spiritually fed. The service would always start with a prayer and the song, He's Sweet I Know. It was at the Church on the Inside that I learned that song and it would get me through many nights in jail and outside of jail.

Sometimes we'd have lock downs. They came as a result of someone having drugs in their possession or anything for that matter that the jail did not issue. A "lock in" is a result of a fight, or an officer trying to gain control of a situation, such as someone getting sick, fights, or just the officer trying to display control. Nevertheless, "lock downs" and "lock ins" were something I did not want to deal with, point blank, unless of course, if it were due to my communicating with the men on the above tier.

I missed my family, especially my baby. But I would say that my first bid was the easiest because, I didn't have any strong vices. By now, Ka'wand is starting to get older. Thank God for my sister, Karen. She became a mother to my son when I was gone. She dropped out of school to take care of him. She wrote to me to tell me that he was always scratching. He had eczema. I didn't know how it had affected him or how he looked because, she didn't send me any pictures of him. I could only dream and imagine how I thought he might look. That's all I could do about it, except pray for him.

I did get a few visits also. Deidra would visit me. Nothing like being inside and not receiving mail or getting visits. It's like life goes on. People forget about you. So because of that, I have only one goal: that's doing my bid. I turned a year older while I was in there. The first of many birthdays on the inside.

Eight months went by and I was released. Mmmm. Can you smell that? Some call it fresh air. I call it freedom. I walked down Carmen Ave. to the bus stop with my belongings in a county issued suitcase: a black garbage bag. I passed Nassau Medical Center and turned onto Hempstead Tpke. I got on the N70 bus. I transferred in Hempstead to the N40 that goes to Freeport. I got off at the Freeport train station and walked to Commercial St. No welcome home party. They were not expecting me. My brother and sisters were in school. I could hear someone in the back of the house and I went back there. There was Karen standing at the sink in the kitchen, washing dishes and a little boy was standing near her.

"Where is Ka'wand?"

"He's right there."

I looked at the little boy on the floor crawling by her feet. I stood there and looked at him. He looked like an old man. Karen said he would scratch so bad that his nails would cause infections on his skin. His skin was scarred from scratching and he looked like his whole body had been burned. He looked up at me. I reached down, grabbed him in my arms and hugged him. He gave me this look like, who is this? He didn't really know me. Karen was the one he knew. It hurt me that he didn't know me but, I understood.

It usually takes experiences for one to make the leap from immaturity to maturity. One sure sign of maturity is the willingness to see to the needs of someone else before your own. The safest experiences are ones learned from others. But generally the most impressionable are our own. The good ones and the bad ones. After her incarceration, April made a concerted effort at taking that leap, from a girl with a baby to a young mother.

A Young Mother Makes A Choice

Aug 1979. By now, I'd been home for about a month. I was experiencing all those things that Karen had told me. This time, I wanted to do the right thing. I really did. I had just gotten out of jail, I had a baby to take care of and I didn't have a job. I didn't want to go back on the stroll. I didn't want to steal, because I didn't want to go back to jail. So, I applied for assistance through the Department of Social Services. I received Medicaid. I also got an emergency needs check worth $40.00. I took Ka'wand to the doctor for his eczema. The doctor prescribed this cream that cost $35.00 and that Medicaid didn't cover. So I took the emergency money and bought the cream so he'd feel better. When I got back to my mother's house, she asked,

"Where's the money, April"

"I used it to buy Ka'wand's medicine. It was $35.00. The check was for $40.00"

"Your sister took care of that baby the whole time you were away. And now you come home and take the money and do what you want to with it."

"He needed his medicine, Madear! You are a mom, what would you have done?"

She's looking at me and I am looking at her...

"You And Your Baby, GET OUT!"

There was a supermarket at the time called Gouz. We had a lot of plastic bags from Gouz stuffed in a cabinet. I opened the cabinet, reached in and started pulling out bags. I then started stuffing

Ka'wand's clothes in them. My sisters were screaming and crying. "Please, Madear, don't do this! What do you mean, get out? Please let her stay!" Begging, they followed my mother into the other room. There was no response. "Then let April go but, please let the baby, stay! Please, Madear!" She never said a word. I knew she wouldn't, so I never stopped to wait for a reply. I packed everything that we had in eight Gouz bags. I had four on one arm, four on the other arm, anything else I could carry in my hands, Ka'wand and a blanket. And I started walking up the street towards Northeast Park. As I turned the corner, I was crying. And I was angry and hurt. I looked up. The sky was so dark and cloudy. I knew that the sky would open up at any minute. I got to the park just as it started to rain. In that moment, I felt like somebody was crying for me. I couldn't find any shelter so I sat down on the ground underneath some bushes and covered our heads with the blankets. I looked down at Ka'wand and I couldn't say anything. I was just sobbing.

"Why me? God, please, why me?"

I was crying and sobbing.

Just then, I heard a lady's voice say, "What are you doing out here, honey? Come in here. Out here with that baby in the rain." Adjacent to the park were the backyards of homes. I didn't realize that I had sat underneath some bushes that were near this lady's yard. I guess she must've heard me crying. I went inside, sat down, and unwrapped the baby. We were both very wet.

"What happened to him?"

"He has eczema"

"Why are you out here in the rain?"

"Madear told me to leave."

I started to cry again. She left the room and came back with towels.

"Well, you and your baby, stay here tonight and tomorrow we'll go down to Social Services."

She took me into the guest bedroom and I put the eight bags on the floor near the bed. I put Ka'wand on the bed and changed his wet clothes. I changed into a gown that she gave me. That night, I slept in the bed with my baby. He scratched all night long. I had an opportunity to see how Karen had to deal with him scratching. I had to keep grabbing his hands and rubbing the area he was scratching. Although he scratched all night, I had a peaceful rest.

The next day, she took me down to Social Services liked she promised. They made a couple of calls and were able to locate a room for me and Ka'wand in a lady's home in Lakeview, NY. Social Services placed us there with a lady named, Ms. Sally*. They paid for the room and gave me food stamps. She was nice to me and always offered to help me with the baby but, I wouldn't let her. A few days passed by and we adjusted to our new environment. One day I was holding him and I said to him, "Look like this where we at right now, K." My baby, my son, looked up at me with those beautiful, big eyes. And then, he wrapped his little scarred arms around me and he held me. In that very moment, I knew that he realized that I was his mom.

Ka'wand's Placement

His skin was so raw from him scratching that it would ooze and then peel off. People who saw him thought he had been in a fire. I know he was in pain from it. It had to hurt. I use to keep him wrapped up all the time because people would look at him and judge me by the way he looked. One day, Ms. Sally caught me off guard and Ka'wand wasn't wrapped up. She gasped.

"What's wrong with that baby? What happened to him?"

"He has eczema"

I explained his history of eczema. That's the least I could do for all that she was doing for us. She seemed to understand what I told her. I thought she believed me but, I found out later I was wrong. One day in early August, she offered to give me a break. I did need a little break I didn't have any money so I went and turned some tricks. I still managed to find time for that. While I was out, she called Child Protective Services. A couple of days later, Ms. Sally and her daughters went out for the day. Soon after she left, there was a knock on the door. I opened it. There standing before me was an attractive white woman with a police officer. He reached over and unlocked the holster to his gun. I found it odd that he'd do that, but I wasn't afraid because I hadn't done anything wrong except turn a few tricks, but that didn't count.

"Ms. Sally is not here. How can I help you?"

"April Cofield?"

"Yes"

"I'm here from Child Protective Services. There have been allegations of child abuse."

"I would never hurt my child. He has eczema. You can call his doctor!"

I was starting to get upset. She started noticing how Ka'wand was looking at me.

"Ms. Cofield, I can see that you love your baby."

"I do! I just don't understand why you're here!"

"In spite of what was reported, I can see something else."

"What do you see?"

"I can see a struggling mother who loves her son."

"Yes"

By now, I'm starting to cry.

"You can't do this by yourself."

"No, I can't."

"You were just recently incarcerated. Let us place him in fostercare."

I looked at her like she had thirty-two heads. I had just had this conversation with my sister Karen and she begged me not to ever put Ka'wand in foster care. "You can take care of him, April! I did the best I could when I had him." I wanted to believe that I could but I couldn't. I was really thinking about Karen. How mad she'd be with me for giving Ka'wand away. The lady kept talking and the more she talked, the more it made sense. I'd been gone for eight months. I have nothing to give him. I don't want him to suffer. By now I'm starting to believe what she has told me.

"But I need to clarify one thing. I just left jail and was in with a woman from Westbury who bashed a baby's head on a porcelain sink. I don't want anybody to hurt him."

"I will make sure that no one will hurt your baby. I promise you that!"

I believed her. I packed his things and gave him to her. He was crying for me as they left and I cried for him. I lay in my room for hours crying. I dreaded calling Karen. When I did, she just cried and cried. She didn't forgive me for a while. I knew that Ms. Sally had turned me in. I was upset with her but, I understood. I stayed with her until I knew for sure that Ka'wand was safe, then I went back to the comfort of Freeport. Back to what I knew best. I wanted to go back to school and all of that but, I hit the streets. I needed to make some money.

They placed him with the first lady. She was too old and had a lot of foster children and Ka'wand was too much to handle with his dietary needs and all. He couldn't drink regular milk. He had to drink goat milk. Next, he was placed with Ms. Johnson* on Seaman Ave. She was so kind to me. She gave me her phone number. "Call me anytime, April. Anytime you wanna see him, you just give me a call." And I was just so grateful that she said that to me. And I did. For a while. He was doing so good there with her. He was happy. I'd go and visit him for a while. Then I'd missed my visits. I trusted her. I knew she'd take care of him.

The social worker that came to take Ka'wand was helping me get myself together as well. She found me another room. I didn't want to stay at Ms. Sally's no more after Ka'wand left. Just too many memories. I was enrolled in BOCES in an alternative program to finish and get my high school diploma. I tried going to school during the day and on the stroll at night. But I finally stopped going to school. The schedule was too much for me and the call of the Dead Presidents was too strong to turn down!

One day, I had this bad feeling that something was terribly wrong. I called Ms. Johnson...

"Please, Ms. Johnson, is Ka'wand alright?"

Yes, baby, he's fine! Don't you worry. He's doing just fine!

I was so grateful to God that she took care of my son. So grateful. After I calmed down, I hung up the phone. And I cried and cried. Cried for what I did. Cried for what I didn't do and then to numb the pain, I got high. I turned to the street a little harder. I started back smoking weed again and this time I started sniffing cocaine. I was no longer paying my rent so by now, I was on the streets again, homeless. And the only way I knew how to make it was through a fair exchange. You give me the money and I'll do whatever you want.

No servant can serve two masters.
For either he will hate the one and love the other;
or he else he will hold to the one,
and despise the other.
Ye cannot serve both God and Mammon.
(Luke 16:13 KJV)

Deep

By now, I'm deep into the game. The customers wanted to be with the new girl. The old timers on the stroll didn't want me there. They'd tell me that I was a baby and should go home. "I ain't a baby." I'd tell them. I watched them as they approached cars and picked up tricks. Some of their techniques worked and some didn't. I picked the ones that worked for me and perfected it. I understood even then that it was all a game. I was still new at it, but I was good.

I started running into my father's friends. The men wanted me but out of respect to my father, most of them didn't ask. The women that caused Madear so much woe looked out for me. They'd see me strolling in front of the C'est La Vie and some of the other clubs on Nassau Road. and they'd say, "Come in here and change your clothes. Knock that off or else do it on the down low." So I did. After that, I started dressing better. I wore my hair in finger waves. My sister, Bobette, could design clothes at an early age. They knew what I was doing. She'd say, "If you gonna be out there, at least you gonna look good!" She once took a ser of red sheer curtains and made me the most beautiful lace outfit. It drew a lot of attention. Made a lot of loot when I wore that outfit with my red heels.

My fees were just enough. I didn't undersell my body or over price it either. But you better believe it was never free. I worked as a public servant (that's what I called it when people asked me my occupation).

"What were your fees?"

"Between twenty-five and fifty dollars. Depended on the type of service I performed." She continued.

I'd start my day early. I'd get up, shower and choose an outfit. I'd get dressed, making sure I was well groomed before leaving the house. I'd take my work bag, which included, Vaseline, condoms, toothbrush, mouthwash, baby wipes, cigarettes, a lighter and a couple of dollars. Later, as things started getting rough out there, I included a body alarm. There were different types but, my body alarm looked like a perfume bottle. If a trick tried to hurt me, I'd point the nozzle in his direction and the piercing noise would frighten them. Anyway, after getting dressed, I'd leave the house and go to the store. I'd buy a newspaper. I'd spread out half of it and sit on it. I'd skim through the other half while observing the street for about forty-five minutes. I would never come to the stroll and take tricks without observing first. I had to make sure that Vice wasn't out trying to make arrests. When I knew it was safe, I would start walking. Back and forth. Back and forth. Stopping only to use the bathroom. I'd stay out there sometimes all night long. There were times when I could work the street for two or three days without a break. Then when I did break, I'd sleep for two days straight. I'd pull long hours but, I had money to take care of myself, pay for my room, buy my weed, cigarettes, and food.

Part of a Deal

A couple of years had passed. I was going in and out of jail for prostitution. Sometimes staying a while and other times released the same day. Ka'wand was still in foster care. I was living my life like I had no responsibilities. Still doing the same things. Hanging out, partying, strolling and getting high. One night I went to this party at Centennial Park in Roosevelt. And this man started staring at me. I didn't pay him any attention because if you don't got the loot, I can't talk to you. He called me over to the car. I went.

"Come here. Got a minute? Can I talk to you?"

"What?"

Cause to be with me, you had to pay me. I wasn't with too many black men. They tried to haggle me down. This ain't Burger King have it your way! If you wanna be with me, release the dead presidents!" Anyway, he said:

"Got some weed. You smoke?" I got in the car. We talked.

"What's your name"

"April. What's yours?"

"Gordon*"

He seemed very nice, but it was important to me that he knew how I made a living. I kept the streets up front. Don't think because you talking to me that I will give up my source of income. Well, we started getting together. I started having feelings for him. He showed me genuine kindness. He was a different kind of man than I was use to. He was a gentleman. He'd light my cigarette and open the door for me. I enjoyed being with him. I even introduced him to Madear. I really didn't put him in the trick category. But don't get it twisted; when he picked me up, he still had to release the dead presidents.

After a while, he disappeared and I didn't see him for about a month. I was gonna write him off. One night late, I was home in the bed and I awoke to all this noise. Sirens. Fire trucks. I looked out the window and saw this man waving at me. It was Gordon. I went down. He had broken the glass on the pole so the alarms would go off.

"April, I've been trying to see you."

Ain't gone lie. I missed him, too. I invited him up. Not as a trick, but as man. My man. After that our relationship took off.

By this time, I had to leave Roosevelt. I moved in with Deidra. I lived at 100 Terrace on the Bedell side. I gave her money for rent. I started strolling in Hempstead. There was a lot of money to be made in Hempstead. Sometimes there'd be ten girls on the street all trying to get in that one car. But there were always plenty of tricks for all of us. This living arrangement worked for a while until she started going down. She started shooting dope. Stopped working and only stayed in the house. I wasn't doing heavy drugs at that time so, I had to leave. I moved back to Madear's house.

I was still seeing Gordon. We were getting together quite often. But then I missed my period and I realized that I was pregnant. I didn't want to keep this baby. I couldn't. How could I bring another child into the world when I wasn't even taking care of my first one? I was plagued with guilt. So Gordon, said, "If you keep the baby, I'll set you up in a place and help get Ka'wand out of foster care."

I could tell he was sincere, so I agreed. He got me a place and helped me get Ka'wand out of foster care. That was one of the happiest days of my life. I was determined that this time, I'd do better. I even stopped strolling for that man. I knew then that I truly loved him. You know it's funny, I never thought about getting married or going to college, I always thought about having a boy and a girl. Pretty soon, I'd have my wish. I was living on Nassau Road in Roosevelt. On December 31, 1981, Ka'wand was in the bed with me and we were watching television. Gordon had stopped by earlier and I was drinking some rum. All of sudden, Ka'wand is looking at me funny.

"Mommy, you peeing in the bed!"

"No, baby! Why you say that?"

Then I looked down and we were lying in a puddle of warm water. The sheets, the mattress, everything was soaked. I called the ambulance. They came and took Ka'wand and me to the hospital. I was in so much pain. It was decided that I needed to have a C-section. The nurses were taking care of my son while I was having the C-section. Then she came. Shortly after midnight. My second gift from God. My beautiful baby girl. Afterwards, in the recovery room, they brought Ka'wand to me. He looked at the baby.

"Mommy, I have a little sister?"

"Yes, baby"

"What's her name?"

"Don-yat"

They let him stay with me and the baby while we all bonded. Later that night as I was resting from the birth, I started thanking God for her life. I wanted her to become someone special. I only secretly wished that the baby was a boy so that there would never be a possibility of her becoming a prostitute like me. I didn't want that life for her. And with those mixed emotions running through my mind, I cried myself to sleep.

So now, I'm twenty years old. Single mother with two children. I want better for them. I want better for me. After a couple of days, we left the hospital. We went back to the apartment on

Nassau Road. It was tough. I was sore from the surgery and had two children to take care of. But Gordon kept his end of the bargain and took care of us. All of us.

Terrace Ave

One morning I was resting with my kids around me and I heard all this noise above us. I opened the door. The owner of the building had sold it to the Eagle* club while me and the other tenant were still there. The Eagle*club were a motorcycle club in Freeport. They were there to clear out the building. I'm a young mother alone with two small children. It was very upsetting. I tried to reach Gordon but, I couldn't so, I had to pack up my things and leave. My life was about to take a drastic turn because after I left Nassau Road I ended up at 103 Terrace Ave Hempstead, NY.

I had lived on Terrace Ave. a while back but, it was different this time. It was unlike anything that I remembered. It was eerie. I thought I had street knowledge, but I really didn't. I can honestly say that I don't think anybody is equipped to deal with what I would eventually endure. Well, we settled in to our new apartment. I didn't have curtains so my neighbors would see me painting the walls. I went and met the neighbors around me. Some were friendly and some were not. I really wanted this to work for us. Only time would tell.

My First Day on Terrace

Terrace Ave. is a street in Hempstead, NY. It is one long block with apartment buildings on both sides. April spent a lot of years living and strolling on Terrace Ave. For the record, there were then and still remain some very decent and hardworking people living there. But like most crime ridden areas, you don't hear much about the good news that comes out of it. Terrace is known for drugs and prostitution. In the spring of 2008, the District Attorney offered deals to known drug dealers that were taped during a surveillance operation.. It was a stay out of jail ticket. The deal was simple. Stop selling drugs and get help through either a rehab center or other supportive services. If not, you'd go to jail.

April wanted to share the experience with me so that I could have a better understanding of the element in which she lived and worked. These were my feelings on my first visit to Terrace.

In Michael Jackson's video, Thriller, the ghouls came out at midnight. Creeping and crawling with worn and tattered clothing and disfigured appendages. In Whodini's, The Freaks Come Out at Night, the lyrics give the image of "freaks" being in all shapes, sizes and colors. The lyrics suggest that the "freaks" weren't disfigured like the images depicted in the Thriller video but ironically they too, came out at night. April described a similar scene that took place daily on Terrace Ave between late afternoon and the early part of the evening. She stated that it was overtly obvious on Fridays, shortly after payday. I imagined they'd trickle in one by one. I was again wrong in my assumption. I met her there on a warm summer afternoon, around 5:00PM. I drove onto the block and spotted her car. I parked behind her. We both got out and greeted each other.

"How goes things, my sister?"

"Things are fine."

"You alright?"

"Yeah, I'm okay."

"Alright. So, let's walk back towards this end of the block and work our way up towards Bedell."

We walked on the left side of the block going towards the Jackson side. We went into the first building. It seemed quiet. She started talking rather loudly, I thought. I'm walking right beside you I wanted to say, but I didn't. I later found out that she did that to let anyone know that someone was walking through so they could stop doing whatever they were doing so we wouldn't have to see.

We kept walking until we came to a set of stairs. We were on the first floor. By the second landing before the next set of stairs leading to the second floor was a window that faced the back of the building. The sun's beams shone through a broken window pane and illuminated dust particles that danced in twirling patterns as the rays were shining through it. April pointed down toward the landing.

"I use to sit here. I would get a newspaper and spread out the back section and sit on it. I would read the first section to see what was going on. Then I'd light my pipe and have my first hit of the day. Mother Todd lived in that apartment. I tried to hurry and get my hit before she came out of the apartment in the mornings. She worked an early shift. I liked her and she liked me. She saw something in me that I couldn't even see in myself."

I listened to her. I knew the story. We went up the steps, passed through the dancing dust particles and went to the second floor.

We continued walking toward the other end until we stopped in front of a door.

"This was my apartment and Ms. Clara's apartment was right here."

I noticed the close proximity of the two doors. Both of them looked the same. Only difference being, one door was a prison to two unsuspecting children, the other, a safe haven. I stood there thinking about some of the stories that she recalled that took place behind those doors when all of a sudden I heard the sound of someone walking toward us. It was a petite lady. She was well groomed with a short, curly hairstyle. Her hair was thin and I could see through it to her scalp which was shining as though she had just recently greased it with some Royal Crown. She was wearing a nice denim outfit and she carried a black purse on her shoulder. We spoke to her. She responded. She and April knew each other. They kept talking. Their voices getting louder as the moving one kept walking. I wondered if she were headed to work and was running late. April must've read my mind. She answered my unspoken question.

"You see her? That's a crack head."

"Where is she going?"

"Outside!"

"But she doesn't look like a crack head. She looks like she just got off work or is going to work."

"Maybe she did, but she's still a crack head."

"How do you know?"

"She's got that walk, Robin"

Still not satisfied with her answer, I add,

"She still doesn't look like a crack head"

"What does a crack head look like, Robin?"

I stopped for a second to think about her question. It dawned on me that in this venue, I am not the resident expert, so I don't know! She stood nearby looking at me, impatiently waiting for me to answer. I can tell that I'm getting on her last nerve. And that if she didn't love and respect me that she'd be telling me off next. Sometimes she can be short tempered. She continues:
"Let's go outside. You'll see. The streets will be full of em."

We walked outside and what was quiet except for the occasional sound of horns blowing or music from an apartment was replaced by a bustling sidewalk with a lot of people walking like they were on a mission. It was Friday. Payday for most, I'm sure. I know what she said but, I refuse to believe that most of these people are crack heads. I know that a lot of them are not! She had told me stories of the ones that prayed for her when she was strung out. Trying desperately to rid my thoughts of the negative images before me, I frantically searched for signs of innocence. And there they were. I saw children playing on the sidewalks and still others were walking from school. I know that even though she might be right, there are also some good people living in this war zone behind enemy lines.

We started up towards Bedell. A beautiful sister in a long dark skirt was walking in our direction. She wore her hair in Goddess Braids. Her eyes sparkled and she had an incredibly beautiful smile. She reminded me of the women I've often seen leaving churches on Sundays with the dollies pinned on top of their heads. Such an angelic face.

"Hello Ms. Cofield"

Hey Dot*, what goes on?"

"Nothing!"

"Taking care of yourself?"

"I'm trying. It's hard but I'm trying"

"God is able. And just remember if nothing changes, then nothing changes."

"I know. You're right. Have a nice weekend."
We walked about five steps, then April said,

"I know what you're thinking, but you're wrong. She's a crack head."

I stopped walking and looked at her.
"Please tell me no!"

"Can't do that. She is Robin."

I'm flabbergasted. I say nothing and continue to walk and look straight ahead.

"What's up partner? What you up to?"

I turned toward her voice and she's talking to a man who has just gone into the hallway of a building. It's very dark in there and several men are standing with the door ajar as she confronts him.

"I'm just getting off work"

"Then why you going in there? Why you not headed home?"

Does she even know this man, I'm thinking? The other men are starting to look at her. They recognize her. Then they look at me; standing nearby, looking all goofy and out of place. She says to him,

"I think you need to keep steppin. You don't want nothing they got."

He's agitated. I'm nervous. Why is she singling him out? He must think she is the police. He comes out of the building and heads in the opposite direction. I didn't like that at all. It made me very uncomfortable.

"D-D-D Did you know him?"

I'm starting to stutter. I do that when I'm nervous, tired, hungry, sleepy. Okay, I admit it! My name is Robin and I'm a stutterer.

"No. but he looks like he not from round here. He needs to go home."

"I didn't see him go in that hallway. All of sudden I heard you speaking to him."

"You didn't see him, Robin?"

"No!"

"You got to be aware of your surroundings, my sister. To be aware is to be alive!"

I know she's right, so I don't respond back, I just keep walking. We approached the corner of Bedell and Terrace. We made a right on Bedell. It's a dead end street, with rows of abandoned houses. There are rental signs in most of the windows. There was a second dead. end to the right. We go there and look out onto the back of Terrace Apartments. It is an open area with a playground on the far end.

"There were many dead bodies found back here. It was also where children would play before they made that playground over there for them."

And I need to see this because? But I dare not vocalize it. I touch my right front pocket for my car keys. My car is starting to call me! Literally! We start to leave and I see these young men across the street. They look like they may be mid to late twenties. They look like some dealers that she described to me. Young and ruthless. They are looking at us. It does appear that we are snooping. I'm very aware of that. Maybe they can even hear her talking to me. She talks rather loudly when she gets excited about things. We crossed the street. They are still watching us. I speak to them by curling up the sides of my mouth while simultaneously nodding my head. Nothing. Not a single one of them spoke to me. Not that it hadn't happened before but usually when someone speaks, it's just common courtesy to speak back. One of them had this look of pure evil in his eyes. Like he didn't give a d--- who we were and would just as soon as take us out for the sheer audacity of making eye contact. We walked until we were on their side of the block and were headed back to Terrace. They were still watching us; trying to figure out who we were. I could feel their eyes boring into the back of my head. I knew in my soul that they were packing.

"*Two women shot on Bedell Ave. gang style see details at 11:00.*"

That's what I imagine the news reporter would say. Now I'm starting to get upset because I didn't want to tell my husband where I went. He didn't want me to come without him. I have got to start listening to him more and stop being so hard headed! The hair on my arms and the back of neck stood up. I wanted to run like hell, but April said,

"Robin, I know what you're thinking; don't do it!"

I didn't run. But if there were any possible way to have an out of body experience, I would've. Because every fiber in my body, my mind and my soul was just as good as in my car with the engine revved, getting the hell up out of Dodge City. All I wanna do is write this book. I did not sign up for this. Now I'm holding my breath and trying to walk in a medium pace. Five more steps. Four more. Three more. In what seems like an eternity, we get to the corner and turn it. Thank you Jesus! Thank you Lord! I'm so thankful to God right now for my life! You just have no idea. Terrace ain't looking so bad to me right about now. After that experience, the worst thing that can happen is someone will think that I'm a prostitute and stop and ask me my fee.

Terrace Ave: The Beginning

We had been there for two years. Gordon wasn't giving me enough money for rent. So I started slinging packages. I was selling weed and cocaine and I would keep some of the money. That was how I paid my rent. I was still smoking weed and sniffing. Everything was fine until a new neighbor moved in. Her name was Mabel*. She and I hit it off. She was a hustler and more street wise than me. I met her because the cocaine that I was selling sold fast. The people on the street were talking about it saying, "You got the good stuff!" Then they would ask me, "Does it come back?" And I'd answer, "Yeah, I guess it does. But what does that mean?" I told the dealer what they were saying. He never explained to me what that meant. He knew what type of people I was dealing with and he'd only say, "April, be careful and be mindful. Remember you have the kids in the apartment." But I was street wise or so I thought. I thought I could handle myself. And I was handling myself until someone told Mabel about me and she became my best customer.

My New Friend:
Crack

One evening, Mabel invited me over. She had a nice apartment. She had a lot of people in there. People with a lot of money. She wasn't in the front room with them. She was in the bathroom and I went to the door and told her that I had to leave and go back home, Don'yat and Ka'wand are at home. She said she'd come by later. So as I'm leaving, I'm looking at what they were doing. They were smoking what I thought was weed but it wasn't, they were smoking these glass pipes. I remember seeing it before. I realized it was freebasing and I immediately thought of Richard Pryor. I remember him saying that it was calling him and I knew that it was something I didn't want to do. I remember thinking I ain't messing with nothing that calls you or makes you want to set yourself on fire! So, as I'm standing there watching them, different ones started asking me,

"Do you smoke, you wanna take a hit?"

"Nahh, I don't do that!"

I didn't know what it was, so I left to go check on the kids.

Mabel came over later that night. She came with her glass pipe and a jar with little rocks in it. White rocks.

"What is that?"

"Whatever you do, April, don't mess with this. Listen to me, I appreciate you being my friend. I adore your kids. But whatever you do, please don't mess with this."

Pretty soon, she left. And the thought of those rocks remained in my head. Indeed it did. Well, even though she said that she didn't want me to mess with those rocks, I was curious about them. So I peeked in on Ka'wand and Don'yat and they were asleep. I figured I would go back over there. I could sniff while they smoked. So I took one hundred of twenty-fives, left the kids and went back to Mabel's apartment. When I got there, the whole apartment was lit up. They were all very paranoid. So I tip toed into the room.

"What you doing here?"

"I wanted to hang out while the kids were asleep?"

She became very frustrated with me.

"April, sit in the kitchen!"

I would find out later that the source of her frustration was the fear that the people in her house would find out that I had the good stuff and instead of coming to her, they'd come directly to me. Thus cutting out the middle man. I didn't know that then, so I went and sat in the kitchen. I started talking to some people that were there. They were smoking and spending money with me. After a while, it was three O'clock in the morning and I went home. The kids were still asleep. I started preparing myself for bed, and then there was a knock on my door. It was Mabel with another person. Harold* and Mabel were close. She was acting really strange.

"Come in and close the door"

She did and handed me a hundred dollars. I gave her four, twenty-five dollar packages. After she had her cocaine, Harold pulled out his.

"Whatever happens, just watch me."

Then she went over to my stove, found a pot and put on some water. She looked in my cabinet. There she found a jar of bullion cubes and dumped the cubes on the counter. She then went in my refrigerator and got some baking soda. I'm standing there watching her, like, what the hell is going on? She then took the cocaine and dumped it in the empty bullion cube jar and added baking soda. She then added water to it.

"Why'd you put water on it? What the hell you do that for?"

I liked to lost my mind! I didn't even have the right to ask her that. She could've blown it in the air if she'd wanted to. That was her stuff. She could've done whatever she wanted to with it. She paid for it! She put the jar inside the pot. And I'm telling you, the most amazing thing happened! That cocaine started to rock up! And then the rocks started jingling! And then she pulled out her glass pipe. It was little and cute. She put a rock in it and lit the bottom and she said,

"All I want you to do is pull on it."

Now, I'm thinking, is she serious? Cause remember, she was dead set against me trying it not even a couple of hours ago. I pulled on that pipe and felt nothing. I did see the cloud go in but I didn't feel anything. She said, "No, you gotta do it again." She then took me in my bedroom and stood me against the wall. Harold followed. She put a bigger rock inside the pipe, she lit the bottom and told me to pull. I did.

My ears started ringing and I felt this tingling through my body and I slid down the wall. And for the next twenty years, that feeling was what I chased! That feeling! That night, I went through a whole five thousand dollar package. I knew the dealer was gonna get me. I remember watching the stories and there was an episode that I used as an alibi. I lied and said that I spilled cool aid on the package. Before he came by, I dumped the empty packages in cool aid. He questioned me but, then he believed me. He then gave me a ten thousand dollar package. He gave me enough for him and for me. And he'd tell me, this is for you and this is for me.

I had enough to live off of if I sold like I was supposed to and not smoke it. At first, I was getting Mabel to cook it for me but then, I learned how to cook it myself. I came to realize that Mabel was grimy. She would cook it and take more than she was supposed to take. I gave her one time to cross me and then it would've been all over. But after, I learned to cook it myself. I didn't need her to cook it for me. Not long afterwards, the word got out. People knew that I sold it and that I didn't have that grimy spirit about me so they started coming directly to me. She didn't like that! She started calling me a cut throat. I wasn't a cut throat, I was a business person. People started talking about me on Terrace Ave. All type of people started calling me. They could trust me. But you have to understand something, there is no honor amongst thieves. Especially crack head thieves. Always remember that. Ms. Clara, my neighbor pulled me aside one day.

"I know that thing that you doing. Bring them kids over here with me."

And I did because it gave me more freedom. She took their clothes. I gave her the food that I had in the house. The kids stayed with her while I did my thing.

Sometimes the kids were with me. But as time went on, things got worse because now I'm opening up my home to an element that I don't want my kids exposed to. I didn't want them to see it, but I couldn't stop. I had people in my living room and bedroom. If my children were home when people came over to smoke crack, I'd lock them in their bedroom. They'd cry and want to get out but I couldn't let them out!

Prostitute Paradise

A whole bunch of transvestites got a hold of my name. They got tired of being a slave to their pimp, Eric* over in Hempstead Heights. Rhonda* had heard about me on the stroll. Rhonda*, was the first one of them that came to my house. She, I mean, he (I was in the habit of calling them she) knocked on my door.

"Hello, you don't know me, but my name is Rhonda*."

"Hello"

"This is for you"

(And he gave me a rock the size of nickel and a fifty dollar bill).

"I know you got kids"

(And he pulled some groceries from behind his back). "You mind if I come in?"

When you went into a crack den you had to pay. Out of respect, that's what you did. So, I introduced him to my children. In a short time, they fell in love with him and he loved them. He treated them like his own children.

News travels fast on the stroll and all the faggots and transvestites came by my house for safety. They'd also come for social gatherings. Just like people have parties and do social drinking, well we'd do social crack sessions. There was Cherry*, Wendy*, Iris*, Dee Dee* and Faggot Kat*. Faggot Kat was the most bodacious one because he had implants. He could stop cars just by stepping outside the door. All the tricks that liked men wanted Faggot Kat. But just like Rhonda, all of them came in bearing gifts for the house.

Most of them would come and stay a short time but Rhonda stayed the longest. He ended up staying for weeks. One day, he said, I'll give you a thousand dollars but all I ask is that you don't open the door. He became very paranoid. I don't know if he ripped off somebody or what. Now I have all of Eric's prostitutes in my house. Months had gone by. But then one morning, there was a knock on my door.

"This is Eric, Ms. AC" I opened the door.

"This is for you"

He gave me money, looked past me and saw all of them asleep. I stepped aside and he walked in.

"Where my money at?"

He started slapping them left and right.

"Yo, you got to chill out! I got children in this house."

He chilled out a little. They didn't leave but, they gave him their money. It was such an intense game. As long as I live, I'll never understand how somebody can work and give their money to somebody else. I soon realized that pimps gravitate to broken spirits. Even in my darkest moments, I was never broken.

My house was changing right before my eyes and I didn't even notice it. I finally realized that Faggot Kat had been stealing from me. I was missing perfume bottles, clothes. How could this be? Easy! Cause I was headed down an even darker and deeper path.

As time progressed, Rhonda and all of them left. I started looking for them because I missed that money. I was also thirsting for crack. Matter of fact, I was worse than thirsty. I'd become like Eric had become to them. So they moved on to the next crack den. My dealer found out about my habit and cut me off. I was now in the apartment with a crack habit and no means to support it.

Soon, Ka'wand's SSI had kicked in because he was considered disabled due to his eczema. I was so strung out. SSI sent me a check for eleven hundred and seventy eight dollars. I spent one hundred dollars on food and medicine for Ka'wand and the rest I spent on crack. I didn't even consider paying my rent.

Muscle Memory

I started noticing a lot of white men going and coming in the hallway. I knew what they were doing. This idea came to my head that I didn't have to wait for anybody to give me a hit. I could make my own money. Go out there and get it myself. And as quickly as I thought about it, the opportunity arose.

My door is closed upstairs but it isn't locked. I checked on the kids and they were asleep. And then I heard it. A familiar sound from the past. I heard the sound of an approaching car turn the corner. And instinctively, my legs knew what to do. I ran outside, told him my fee, hopped in that car and took care of that man. I got twenty five dollars from him. (she snaps her fingers) Just like it never left me. And the ironic part was, I didn't have a thing in my refrigerator unless you want to count the plastic milk jug that was filled with water. That was all I had. I knew that Ms. Clara was gonna feed my kids when they woke up. So, I went down to the other side of Terrace Ave. There was a lady there name, Ms. Janie". She sold drugs. I knew she was gonna hit me off. I got down there and gave her my money and she looked

at me.

"So you done went that route?"

She said looking at me sadly.

She didn't wait for me to answer. She knew. Everybody knew that the transvestites and faggots were sleeping in my house and paying me money. People use to come over to the house. They'd eat. It was peaceful. It wasn't that crack den mentality. Yet everyone knew that you don't hang out at AC's or Ms. Cofield's house for free. People talk on the streets. So, she also knew when they left.

Anyway, she felt sorry for me and gave me seventy dollars worth of cocaine for the twenty five dollars that I gave her. Trying to limit the number of times I'd sell my body. I was thankful for her generosity, but it didn't stop me from doing what I do best. Now I'm back on the stroll, with two kids to take care of. But this time, I'm driven by an addiction that was stronger than anything I'd ever been up against in my life.

No Place for Kids

I continued leaving my children with Ms. Clara and she would take care of them while I was out on the stroll. I was driven to make the money now more than ever. I still took care of my body. I didn't look like a lot of women on the stroll. Most of them had missing teeth. I swore I'd never look like that. Never look like them. I developed a clientele like the one I had when I was younger. Ka'wand was in school during the day. As soon as he'd leave for school, I'd leave to turn tricks to pay for my crack habit.

I did this every day. That was my nine to five job. I made a lot of money but I wasn't paying my bills. Soon, they started piling up. After a couple of months of not paying my light bill, my lights were turned off. Not long after my landlord knocked on the door. He was there with the sheriff to pack up all my stuff. I had seen the eviction notices but, I didn't pay it too much attention.

Child Protective Services was downstairs to take Ka'wand, because he had previously been in foster care. They didn't take my daughter because, I told them I'd call her father and he would come to get her. Don'yat and I started crying as they drove away with Ka'wand. I thought about all those times when he just wanted to be with me like a child should want to be with his mom. Then, I started thinking of all the times I had denied him that chance because I was in the street. That thought stabbed me like a knife. That was one of the worst days of my life.

There was a lady who lived in the next building. She knew what happened to me and my kids. She said, "Let your daughter stay here." I wanted her to stay with Ms. Clara but now, I can't trust her. I think she might've called protective services. I left my daughter with the lady and went into the hallway and got high.

The next day, I called Gordon. He came to get Don'yat and took her to Queens with him. She cried as he took her from my arms.

News of my trouble spread quickly. I found out later that it had been Ms. Clara that made the phone call to child protective services. I was so upset that she did that, but I guess she was getting tired, too. They weren't her kids. She was helping me out. Doing me a favor. If it hadn't been for her, the county would've taken them sooner.

With no where to go, I had to find a crack den to sleep in. Most of my stuff had to be put in storage. I was now officially a homeless crack head prostitute. Running the streets. Working two or three days straight. Crashing in a crack den when I needed sleep. Working and sleeping then thinking about my children. Crying for what I couldn't do for them or give them. And getting high to ease the pain. Even though I didn't take care of them like they meant the world to me, they did. I'm just sorry I couldn't show them. I wanted more than anything to keep them with me so I could at least see them. But not like this. I started praying to God asking him,

"Take them back!"

"Take them back, Jesus!"

"I can't take care of them. I don't know where Ka'wand is" "So, I give them both back to you!"

"And if you see fit. If you see fit, Jesus, bring them back to me!"

AI kept crying and praying and soon, I left the hallway, went to a crack den on Terrace, found a spot on the floor among other homeless crack heads and cried myself to sleep. I woke up the next morning. My first thoughts were of them. My children. I realized that I wasn't in my apartment with them. I found my pipe, lit it and numbed my pain.

About a month had passed and I was getting worse. I wasn't taking care of my hygiene. I wasn't combing my hair. My clothes were nasty and I smelled. I looked like s--t. But you know what? It never slowed down my business. One day, I was out working the stroll and this new car pulled up. I figured it had to be somebody I knew because they were approaching me and had already driven by some other girls. I also knew that it wasn't an undercover. I got in the car and this child threw her body up against me and wrapped her arms around my neck. I realized it was Don'yat. I started crying. I didn't want her to see me out here. I didn't want her to see me like this!

"Why did you bring her out here?"

"She's been crying for you, April."

He looked tired and exhausted.

"She's been crying for a whole month. She cries herself to sleep. She wakes up, realizes you aren't there and cries some more. I've tried everything! I just don't know what else to do. She wants to be with you!"

"Mommy, please let me be with you! I miss you! I wanna sleep in my own bed. I want my brother!"

"Why did you bring her here?"

He didn't answer me.

I looked down at my daughter. She was so beautiful. Her skin was so soft. My eyes couldn't get enough of her. I held my baby as she cried for me. I cried for her. I smelled her hair and her skin and clothes. Then, I kissed her forehead and her hair, being careful not to put my mouth too close to her face. I hugged my baby girl and reached for the door handle. As I opened the door, I could hear her screaming as loud as she possibly could. Calling my name; the one name I always wanted to hear:

"Mommy!"

I quickly slammed the car door and ran and jumped into a familiar trick's car. I quickly serviced him and got out with my loot. I ran to get some crack. I needed to numb my pain.

By now my life consisted of strolling and smoking crack. I would lay my head down just a minute when I could. It really didn't matter where. I couldn't go to Madear's. She was dealing with her own addiction. Besides, I needed to be near the street that provided the income that would pay for the crack I smoked daily.

Downstairs from my old apartment was a crack den. It was very convenient like a corner store. I didn't use it often but, I knew it was there if I needed it. This particular day, I went there to check it out. I needed a place to sleep but, most importantly I needed my first hit of the day. That's when I saw the crackhead's baby. As I held him, I knew that I couldn't stay there. It reminded me of all that I wasn't doing for my own children. I could buy crack from her, but I couldn't stay.

*Therefore, thus saith the Lord God:
Because thou hast forgotten me and cast me
behind thy back, therefore bear thou lewdness and
thy whoredoms. (Ezekiel 23:35KJV)*

Jailing

Over the course of seventeen years, April had numerous arrests that lead to twenty-nine convictions. Some of the arrests only amounted to desk appearances. The penalty for some of the convictions was as short as thirty days and the longest terms were for a year. She had a felony charge that was expunged from her record because she was a minor. As an adult offender, she was arrested on four felony counts but, was convicted of two. Her felony charges were for possession of a controlled substance. The bulk of her arrests were for prostitution. Her detailed criminal report is long enough to wall paper an entire room! Imagine that! For testimonial purposes it's not important to cover each individual arrest and conviction. I wanted you to know just how many times April had been a resident in the Nassau County jail. Only a few of the arrests will be discussed.

My longest time served was a year, but I would get four months off for good behavior. It is called a "county bullet." A county bullet is a term used by those in the system to describe the actual term served. I served four county bullets. My first bid was a county bullet and the other three were for possession of a controlled substance.

My shortest time served was thirty days but of the thirty, I served twenty days, allowing ten days of good behavior. Most of the short times were for prostitution. If Mineola Vice picked me up, then I was given a misdemeanor which was a ninety day sentence, of which I served sixty days.

I was a known prostitute and when I got caught, Mineola vice didn't like me because if they put decoys out I would warn the tricks. "Don't pick her up!" Then Mineola Vice would book me for obstruction of justice. I'd get thirty days and have to pay a two hundred and fifty dollar fine. Most of the tricks never served time because they would pay the fine, because they didn't want to be exposed nor have their wives find out.

Whenever I was arrested, I never gave the arresting officers any problems. When they arrested me, I knew that I'd get some rest, I'd have three meals, and a bed.

"It is such a pleasure to arrest you, Ms. Cofield."

I was alright with the police cuffing me. God used it to rescue me from myself. How you gonna sell your body and you ain't even washed it? Just the thought of it made me wanna get high and I did.

I would usually get assigned to the Drug and Alcohol Rehabilitation tier also known as D.A.R.T. The D.A.R.T. dorm became my home away from the streets for a large part of those years.

When I first went to jail, women wore blue dresses. They were below the knee and made out of cotton. It was odd to see the bull daggers wear dresses on the inside and they wore suits on the outside better than most men. Now the women wear dark green scrubs. Some of the ladies had T-shirts or sweatshirts to wear underneath their uniform, because it is so cold in jail.

The women use to have church services in the laundry room when I first went to jail. It was in these services that I started reading the word of God. We were then allowed to have coed church services in the chapel with the men. Those coed services lasted for about three years. They stopped having coed services after an inmate got pregnant.

My shortest release time was eight hours. I was released in the morning and was back in jail the same day. I felt like an idiot! I know it was a trap and I fell hard. I was released and I walked down Carman Ave. headed toward Hempstead going back to Terrace Ave. I was almost on Terrace and I saw this man in a car watching me. He pulled up.

"Yes? Can I help you?"

"I'm looking for a date"

"I might be able to help you with that."

I looked up the block and down the block. I didn't see the Police so I got in the car. Now mind you, I had just gotten out of jail and I usually start my day by checking out the scene to make sure there were no decoys around. It looked safe.

"Let's drive over by the bus station"

I knew, then that he had done this before. Maybe that was where he took his dates. I didn't want to leave the comfort of my turf.

"No. Give me the loot and we'll pull over right here."

He was hesitant but, he didn't want me to get out of the car, either. Well as soon as I took the money, an officer that I knew very well pulled up.

"Hello April. What you doing?" He knew.

"Sitting here talking to my old friend."

"Oh yeah? Then you should know each other's name, right?" Damn. I don't know this man's name. The officer leaned in the car and asked him.

"So what's her name?"

"April"

Whew! He heard the officer say my name when he spoke to me. I start looking around inside the car for something, anything with this man's name on it.

"That's good. Sounds like he really is your friend. But April" The officer was looking at me and I could feel it. I answered him.

"Yes"

"What's his name?"

Damn. I'm busted and I know it. Like a deer in headlights, I answered him,

"John"

Stupid! Out of all the names to choose from, I go and say "John!" The man didn't even look like his name was John.

"Okay John. Let me see your license."

He reached in his wallet and gave the officer his license. The officer looked at me. I knew what his next words would be.

"April, you're under arrest for-"

He opened the door and I got out. I turned around and he put the handcuffs on me. By this time another officer had pulled up on the scene and was talking to my date. Later that afternoon, I was arraigned and placed in a holding cell in new admit, all within eight hours of getting out. Sandy, the coordinator of the D.A.R.T. Dorm couldn't believe it.

"April, you just left this morning!"

I was still in a state of shock. My clothes that I'd just turned in had not been sent down yet to be washed for another newbie. They sent me down the bag of clothes that I had just pulled off that morning and I put them back on. I was in for another thirty days for prostitution. That only happened once. Never again.

The Bearer of the Torch

On a few occasions while I was incarcerated, I was placed in the J and K dorms. There were different speakers who came in to talk to us. One day this woman came in. She introduced herself to the group. Her name was Pam. I'd heard about her but now was able to put a face to the name. She started talking about what she use to do and what she was doing now. I wanted to be free like that but, I knew that only Jesus could do that for her. I was wondering if He could do it for me.

Usually after a meeting the attendees go up to the speakers to thank them and just talk to them. I didn't go up to her. I sat in my seat and watched as everyone else went up to Pam and thanked her. All of sudden, she pointed at me.

"You! April Cofield! Let me tell you some things."

I looked at her and thought, "I know this dope fiend hooker is not talking to me!" I got up anyway and went to see what things she wanted to tell me.

"I've heard about you and I want you to know that it don't have to be this way. When you get out, you can come with me to my church. Memorial Presbyterian Church."

I knew the church she spoke about. I'd walked by it and driven by it with my dates.

"Whatever"

"I mean it. You can!"

That would be my one and only conversation with Pam. I was in the company of greatness, yet my stuff would not let me see it. I would later learn the importance of her significance in my life and why those few words would one day come back to me and help put together the pieces of a puzzle.

April told me that for most of the time while she was incarcerated, she didn't get visitors. I understood that oh too well. Even though my family had been raised in the church and loved the Lord with their whole hearts and soul, a lot of them didn't believe in visiting our incarcerated family members. There are many other families that share that same belief.

I'm sure in a lot of cases, the families were tired of being lied to. Tired of making excuses and taking up the slack for them while they were "Away". If they were known for having sticky fingers or had a drug habit, tired of having to watch their family member's every move and take inventory of personal items after they were gone. Maybe one or all of the above were reasons why April's family visited so rarely. I don't know; I didn't ask them. Just remember, there are two sides to every story. A lot of families are thrust into this defense mechanism, so who am I to judge? I still wonder, though, if they know the verse from Matthew 25:36 that says we should feed and clothe our hungry, visit our sick and visit those in prison. I had never read the verse until I started meeting with April. As she started telling me how it felt, I couldn't help but think about my own incarcerated family members that I never visited.

Commissary

Commissary: a portable store in jail where inmates can purchase snacks and personal supplies.

I didn't really get commissary when I was in jail. My family or friends sent me letters, but no one sent me money to purchase snacks and other things. I had to learn how to jail! I would play spades and other mind games. I would bet the other inmates whatever they had and most of the time, they'd lose.

I did get a card once from my mother and my little sister, La-toya. They sent me a birthday card and inside was a twenty- five dollar money order. I didn't use it to purchase commissary, I saved it so when I got out I could buy crack.

There were many memorable experiences inside the jail. The most memorable one was that I received news of my son.

But we glory in tribulations also; knowing that tribulation worketh patience; and patience, experience; and experience, hope:
(Romans 5:3-4KJV)

News of My Son

I didn't like to sit around and wait for my bid to be over. I would take classes. Anything that I thought would help me. I would take GED courses but I didn't complete it while I was in jail. I would sit in on the bible study classes and take parenting classes.

I learned what was normal for parents. We saw films of how we should behave as parents. We spent a lot of time in discussions. We would discuss what we did to our children and sometimes I felt that they were there to find out more about us than to teach us. It was there that I was forced to face what I couldn't when I was high on crack. Up until now, I haven't seen Ka'wand for seven years. I didn't know who had him. I knew nothing. I started asking questions of women who I knew were there for hurting children.

"Did you see a boy. A little boy there name Ka'wand"

I had to ask them why they would hurt their children. I really started praying more at that point. I don't know if I really trusted God, but I kept praying anyhow.

One of my parenting instructors asked us to write our names down on the questionnaire. I wrote down my name. He looked at the name and then looked at me.

"What's your name?"

"April Cofield"

"Oh, my God!"

I looked at him. He looked like he was crying.

"Can you stay after?"

"I'm not allowed to stay after."

He got up from his seat and went to the officer. They exchanged a few words. I don't know what he said but, they gave me permission to stay behind. Everyone else left the room and it was just he and I.

"April, I want to tell you something that I could lose my job over."

"Okay"

I can't imagine what he could possibly say to me that is so important and worth losing his job over.

'I work at this place called St. Agnes*."

"What's that?"

"It's a home for boys."

"Okay."

"Well there's this bright eyed little boy there named Ka'wand." I feel like I've been knocked in my chest and I hardly have enough air to say:

"That's my son!"

He started crying, I started crying and I kept saying:

"That's my son! That's my son!"

After some time he said,

"In his file, it says he has no known relatives."

"Oh yes, he does. He has a grandmother! He has me! He has a lot of aunts!"

"But in his file, it says he doesn't have family. He's a ward of the state, April."

I quickly wrote down my mother's name and number. He called her. My mother gave the information to my sister, Bobette and she started visiting him. Bobette let everyone know she was his aunt. She would visit him and take pictures and send them to me. I found out later that he was up for adoption. But most people didn't want an older boy. At the time, he was between ten and twelve years old. Some families wanted him but they didn't have the history of his eczema. They couldn't just go to Nassau Medical center and get his records. I was so glad to know where he was.

Couple of months later, I was released. You would think that I'd go see my son, but I didn't. I couldn't go see my son. I had all that time to think about him and was thankful to Bobette for visiting him but one fact about me remained: I was still a crack head and the addiction still controlled my life. So I got out and I went deeper to the street. I thought about him while I was out there. I always did. I felt relieved though, that he was alive. Because prior to that I didn't know whether he was dead or alive.

I had told April that I wanted to go into the D.A.R.T. dorm. It was arranged that I could go in with her on a Monday evening. She goes in every Monday to have bible study with a faith group that she started. Then afterwards, she moves into the dorm to offer encouragement to the entire D.A.R.T. dorm.

I was nervous that day. I'd never been in a jail before. We had to walk through numerous gates with an escort until we reached the dorms. The seats were situated in a large circle. Everyone took a seat. I sat next to a young woman who was there with a baby. She had the baby stroller, bottles, diapers and all. April started talking to the ladies and she introduced me. I said "Hello". I was listening to April but I was fascinated by the fact that there was a mother inside the prison with a baby. It was a young baby. It started to cry a little and the new mommy picked her up. Others sitting near her wanted to help. They were probably thinking of their own children. Ones they'd left outside.

I wanted to take in everything! So I turned my attention from the mommy with her baby to everything and everyone else. There were women of all ages and races sitting in the circle. Some of them had battle wounds that were clearly visible, others had safely tucked theirs away in a place where no one could see them. I looked beyond the circle of women to the walls lined with doors. Some of the cells had single beds and others had doubles. There were washers and dryers and three tables. One had a chess board printed on the top surface. I looked up and there was light coming in through a big skylight. It was a summer afternoon, so the natural light gently enveloped the space and warmed the faces of the women. We could've easily been any other place, but as my gaze dropped and I looked at each woman dressed in green, I knew I was not. I slid down in my chair a bit. First mistake. Never give a tired person an inviting chair. I was getting sleepy. The next thing I remembered was coming to. I don't know how long I was gone but it was peaceful. Later when I tried to tell others that I dozed off in the jail, they couldn't comprehend how that might be possible. April often said that the jail rescued her each time she was incarcerated. After my nap on the inside, I understood the probability of that statement.

*For ye are bought with a price: therefore glorify
God in your body, and in your spirit,
which are God's.(1 Corinthians 6:20KJV)*

The Stroll

April and I met at my home and drove to Oyster Bay for a hotdog and Italian ice at Bonanza. It's a small red shack on a corner in the village square. Small and unassuming, but sometimes the line is around the corner. They make the absolute best hotdogs with chili. They also serve sixty one flavors of Italian ice. We order four hotdogs, steak fries and two large lemon ices. We then drove to the Theodore Roosevelt Park and sat by the water to watch the boats come in and go out. Some of the boats are making pleasure trips but a lot of them are harvesting clams.

I found a nice spot to park the car where we'd be able to have a nice view of the bay. We divided up the steak fries, hotdogs and Italian ice, blessed the food and start to eat. I turned on the tape recorder. In between bites, April answers my questions about the stroll.

Most of my clients, I'd service in their cars. They all knew how good I was at what I did and would wait for me. Sometimes, I'd have cars lined up ten deep or more waiting for me to do one. Finish. And do the next.

One day I was out on a busy day with the cars lined up down Franklin Ave. I serviced the men, quickly and efficiently. Giving each man his money's worth. I never slacked off on the job.

Anyway, by the time I got to the last car, he tipped me for my quick service. I never worried about them being with the other girls when I was on the stroll.

"Tell me your fees again?"

"Depends. Twenty for a blow job and forty for a lay"

"How much time for each service?"

"Five minutes or less"

"What if they wanted both?"

"That's called a half and half. That's sixty bucks"

"For ten minutes?"

"No! Still for only five minutes!"

"That ain't no discount!"

"You sound just like the brothers that use to come on the stroll. That's why I didn't mess with too many of them. Always trying to haggle me down. This ain't no Burger King have it your way! This is business! Had a brother one time ask me, what can I get for one hundred dollars?"

"You get a half and half and the rest is my tip!"

I had to ask her:

"Tip? How you gonna work for five minutes and then ask for a tip?"

"Don't people get a tip when their service is good?"

I didn't answer. She finishes her point.

"If the service is good, you expect to get a tip."

I accept that answer and go to my next question.

"Did you ever fall in love with a trick?"

"Didn't have time for that. My regulars knew what I did. That was part of the excitement for them. Had one regular though, wanted to take me to the movies. I said: "A movie?"

"Naahh! I don't think so, partner. You can just pass me the dead presidents. The money you spending on a movie, popcorn and soda can be in my pocket."

If we confess our sins, He is faithful and just to forgive us our sins, and to cleanse us from all unrighteousness. (1 John 1:9KJV)

A Woman's Worth

I stopped the recorder. All of these thoughts are flooding my mind. I feel as though I am having a panic attack. I start to breathe deeply through my nose and out through my mouth to minimize the anxiety. April's response to my questions brought up feelings that I had never experienced before. Things that I thought I'd laid to rest were now heavy on my heart.

She looked at me with concern in her eyes and asked me, "You alright?" I shook my head "No." And then I told her. I shared some things that I'd done in my past. Some things that I wasn't proud of. No! Things that I was downright ashamed of. Some of them were buried so deeply beneath my present station in life that I'd forgotten about them. Now don't get me wrong, I'm not saying that I should carry it around like a noose around my neck, but how easily we forget! All of these thoughts are running through me, but the one thought that resounded more loudly than all others was the question: What is a woman's worth?

People look at April and judge her based on the fact that she sold her body for a living. But what about those of us that gave it away for free? What about us? Did she love herself more than I did? Did she have more self-respect because at least she had good enough sense to get paid to do what some of us were doing for a meal at Red Lobsters, maybe? Some of you are saying, "Not me!" Well I beg to differ. If you received gifts of jewelry, clothing, money, favors, gotten bills paid etc. and freely parted your knees, then you may need to rescind your response.

On previous rides, it was I who comforted her. This time, I needed comforting. She looked at me and recited 1" John 1:9. That verse was exactly what I needed to hear. I am thankful at that moment that she attends bible study every week and has the ability to recall scripture from memory. I don't do either but, I have got to do better.

She continues to try and calm me down. And I know that she is right, but the self-righteous hypocrite part of me wants another answer. I picked up my bible and I frantically searched for the verse. I dare not ask for help or else I'd have to explain and expose yet another one of my shortcomings.

"Please let it be her. Let her sin be worse than mine so I can feel better about what I did."

I searched and I searched but would not find comfort in the word to whitewash my sin. I'm ashamed to say so! So I confess.

"Yes! I did it! I kissed the frogs knowing full well that they were not princes. In comparison, they were not even royalty and I knew it! Whether I loved them or lusted for them, the act that I committed with them was wrong. They were all tricks, just like April's. I willingly assisted them in tricking me into thinking that it was okay. I've never asked before, but I humbly come now and say: I am truly so sorry for what I did. Please forgive me, Lord."

Occupational Hazards

We met that following Friday afternoon. We drove to our favorite spot and sat there by the water's edge, looking out over the Bay and watching the setting sun. It was playing a game of hide and seek as it sought out a safe haven to sleep until the next morning. April continued where she left off from the previous week.

There was another time when I went out with this black man. I knew better, because like I said, I don't usually go out with black men. This particular night it was busy. They want too much for that little bit of money they give out. This black man rolled up and I guess he recognized that most of the folks out there were men. He stopped.

"How much for a blow job?"

Cause of Reagonomics, I had to go up on my fees.

"Thirty dollars"

"Get in"

"Ima want my money when I get in"

He gave me the money. You know, that's something about me, I may not have remembered what all the tricks looked like but I could tell what bills he gave me. How many hundreds. How many fifties. How many tens. It's always all about the loot. Anyway, I got in and I parked him on Cathedral Ave. You see, black men would take forever with a blow job and then they wanted sex and not give you any more money. Well, I'm taking care of him and he's taking a long time. If I'm in the car with you more than ten minutes that's too long. Else you reaching back in your pocket or I'm getting out of the car. So, I rest for a minute. Is this working for you? He hauled off and swung and hit me in my eye. "You that bitch, April. I heard about you when I was upstate."

I'm thinking as my eye is swelling up; Fight! By now I'm leaning back against the door and I'm kicking and screaming. I'm not using my hands because I got my hands on the money. As I'm screaming and yelling, I'm trying to open the door to roll up out of that car. I'm screaming and yelling but not leaving without the money. I manage to open the door. And as I'm getting out of the car, I see lights coming up behind us. He pulled off. I'm on the ground now and my eye is shut. Police Officers are looking

at me.

"April what are you doing back here?"

I'm looking at them. They know what I'm doing back here. They went on to say that the residents of the building heard someone screaming and called the police.

"You want to go the hospital?"

"No, I don't want to go to no hospital."

I just wanted to get high. I got back on the block and everybody asked me, "What happened to you, Ms. Cofield? What happened A.C.?" I told them. They were shocked. They know that I don't usually mess with black men. Usually. But this night the only color I concerned myself with was green. Well, 1 can't go back on the stroll like this and I can't stay in a crack den, so I go back to Madear's house. I stayed there two days until the swelling went down and my eye wasn't black no more. I healed and went back on the streets to work. Maybe a month later, I was on the stroll and I'm standing by the light, this black man pulled up. He's waving money at me. I ignore him. He circled the block and came back. I get in the car. He can't talk but he shoves money in my hand.

"I want a blow job and a twenty."

"Twenty of what?"

"Some crack"

He wanted some crack. I looked at him. Oh my God, this can't be! This is that fool that opened up my face and somebody done turned him onto crack. Can't be! So I said okay. I had him turn around. I took him over to Bedell and Terrace. He turned around to park and I got out to get the crack. I went in the building and saw some of my male friends.

"See that fool out there in that car?"

"Yeah, AC"

"Well he's the one that opened up my face"

They went outside. Next thing, I hear him screaming like a woman. After a little while, I hear him driving off. They came back upstairs and handed me some crack. They also had a big old wad of money. I didn't see him no more after that!

The Right Choice

Another time I went on Cathedral Ave. to service my client. As he was handing me over my money, I heard some footsteps. I looked up near the apartments and I saw someone climbing the fire escape and go into a window. I knew the person was up to no good. Just as we were about to start, the cops pulled up. I get out of the car. One of em asked me,

"April, who are you in the car with?"

"A friend of mine"

"Oh, really?"

"Yeah, a friend of mine! Why are you standing here asking me about my friend, you should check out that man that just climbed the fire escape behind the apartments!"

He looked at me as though he was deciding which was more important: to collar a prostitute and her trick or check out what I'd told him. He knew I was telling the truth.

"April, this better not be a joke!"

"Why would I lie about that? He just went in that window!"

"And you and your friend better leave from here!"

He went to investigate what I'd told him. We left the block. A couple of weeks went by and I saw that same cop again. He didn't give me the details but, he thanked me for helping to save a lady's life.

The Commandeer

Commandeer: to take over someone else's property as though it is yours.

Not long after that I met this lady name Joyce* who was a crack addict. She lived to get high but, she held down a regular job. She had an apartment. I started getting high with her. Pretty soon, I moved into her apartment. I fed her crack habit and slept there for free. After a while, I invited other people to join me at her apartment.

We made sure Joyce had everything she needed. We would hustle up money to keep on the lights and we took over that apartment. All we had to do was feed her crack. The place was ours. We kept her so high that she stopped going to work. She barely left her bedroom. Pretty soon we had to leave there as well. Just like me, she had been evicted.

I eventually turned out many people to crack just as Mabel had turned me on to crack. I also started having base dates. These are dates where they pull up, they ask your fee, and ask can you get some crack. I liked having base dates. I always got my loot up top. And most of the time once they got high, they couldn't perform. So basically, I got paid to get high.

We took over 115 Terrace. People would be in there paying rent and we were in there like it was ours. Drug dealers tried to find us. I had the top floor. People didn't call me Ms. Cofield anymore, they started calling me "Legend". The little boys would hear them talking about me. That was difficult for me because they knew Ka'wand.

Things got hectic. You could take a broom, touch a ceiling and somebody's package would fall out. We owned Terrace Ave. The game got rough. Some of the boosters would go over to Abraham and Strauss on Hempstead Tpke, and steal a whole rack of clothes, then bring it to Terrace Ave. that's why that store closed down. By now, I'm starting to display leadership skills. I rounded up a group that we named the "Beam Team".

The Beam Team

I have always been a leader, not a follower. You just couldn't step to me any kinda way. Some of the drug dealers were starting to do just that. So, I gathered a team of base heads and formed a group. I worked the outside of Terrace. Around the perimeters.

The people that joined the team with me were doctors, lawyers, nurses and teachers. They had money and they smoked plenty of crack. We were called the Beam Team. Our mission was to turn every drug dealer or as many as possible into crack heads. They acted like they were doing us a favor and could talk to us any old kinda way. I had to tell one:

"Check this out!"

"I'm the one that just finished nodding my head to this."

"You ain't talking to me like that."

"Watch how you talk to me. Cause I ain't having it!"

"Yeah I'm a prostitute. Yeah, I smoke crack!"

"But you not gone talk to me like that and not call Ms. Cofield."

He said, "You a bitch,"

"Then call me Ms. Bitch,"

I decided that I was tired of the drug dealers disrespecting me. Disrespecting us. Through much perseverance and hard work, we were able to get a few of them.

I soon met a trick with connections that told me about the beam. He said if you walk between the fire hydrant and the light poles and break the beams, the lights would come on. Then I started watching while I was strolling and sure enough each time that happened, the lights would come on and if you looked up while walking through the pole and the hydrant, you could see the camera.

For those that had the money to pay for the information, I would tell them about the cameras on Terrace Ave. Some had the nerve to ask me:

"Where's the beam? How you know about the cameras on Terrace? You the police?"

"Nah, I ain't no daggone police and if I was the police just cause of your attitude I'd have you locked up."

One female Jamaican drug dealer came on the scene and said to

me:

"Ms. Cofield. Me like you. Me like you, Ms Cofield. But me hear you Po po."

"I don't care what you heard. I got dead presidents you want'em or not? I'll keep stepping to the next one. Somebody gone sell me something."

For the life of me, I can't understand how they never knew. I can't understand how they were in the game so long and never knew. I'll tell you how? They knew how to market and sell drugs, but had no common sense. Something like that is obvious to a duck! We couldn't get no UPS, cablevision, pizza delivery or anything during those times. None of that stuff. So every time I saw one of those trucks, I knew it was undercover.

The game went on and got vicious. The dealers were ruthless. They didn't play. Some of the girls on my team ended up dating one or two of em. And I didn't see them no more after that. If I did, they would have a crack smile. That's when the drug dealer would take a razor and cut them on one side from the ear to the mouth. It looks like a smile when it heals.

The remaining members of the Beam Team were still diligently working on the job. Smoking and trying to make more crack heads. After some time, we had to dismantle as most of them were too cracked out to work or no longer cared.

I did learn a valuable lesson during that time. You can't help everybody. I realized that after I was labeled a snitch. Some of those same people that I warned about the beams between the poles started saying I was a snitch. How is it I can be a snitch and I always end up in jail? I know a lot about what goes on. Most prostitutes know a lot about what goes on but now, my life was in jeopardy.

Well I got to a point where I couldn't trust anybody. So I made a few new friends that I introduced to anyone that stepped to me wrong. They were Smith and Wesson. Because the drug dealers and tricks were getting grimy. Some of the prostitutes ended up dead out on those golf courses. It wasn't gonna be me! Ever! Time was not my friend on Terrace Ave. I still didn't know where my son was and my daughter was with Gordon. I was always in the hallway at 145 Terrace Ave. I'd take care of my tricks. Then I had money to buy drugs and eat. Afterwards, I would sit on the stairwells. It was quiet there. It was peaceful for me.

The Ones that Prayed for me

Sometimes, I'd be coming in on Sunday morning just as my old neighbor would be leaving to go to church. She would say,

"April, God has something for you to do. And I'm gonna keep praying for you until you do it!"

I never answered and never disrespected her. I was tired from working the midnight shift so, I just kept it moving.

There was another lady named Mother Todd*. That's what I called her, Mother Todd. She would be up early in the morning at 4:00AM. I would hear her because I would be up with my newspaper, my crack and my crack pipe. I would sit on the steps and I would hear her getting ready for work. I would hurry and take my hit before she came out of her door, so I wouldn't be so paranoid when I saw her.

"April, anytime you need to wash your face, brush your teeth or want a drink of water you can knock on my door."

"Thank you Mother Todd."

"You are so beautiful. You don't have to subject yourself to these things April."

Sometimes, I wanted to wash my face and hands. I guess I felt like I looked.

"Mother Todd, can I wash my face and hands?"

"Sure, April. Come on in. You can shower too if you want to."

I never did though. I would turn tricks and hit the streets. Another older lady in the complex would see me.

"April, when I hear your heels a clicking, I start praying for you."

This always made me want to cry. Cause even during this time when I was at my lowest point, God had dispensed angels to watch out for me.

Encounter with Infamous Serial Killer

One evening this white van pulls up on the stroll. I didn't recognize it but I knew it wasn't an undercover. He stopped near me and I opened the door and got in.

"It smells in here!"

He appeared to be agitated. He wasn't responding fast enough. Time is money.

"Are we gonna do this?"

"I got a room at the Shapri"."

"I ain't got time for no room. You got the loot? You want a blow job? What you wanna do?"

At that moment Faggot Kat walked by. Faggot Kat was the man with the breast. He said,

"I want her"

"Okay. You want her? Fine! But I ain't getting out til you give me the loot."

He gave me $25.00 just to get out of the truck. I got out and walked back to the sidewalk.

"Hey Katherine, this cracker wants you!"

"Alright, A.C. I'll hit you up later."

When a girl turns over a trick to another girl, you pay them a little something. Either money or drugs but you give em something. A couple of days passed and next time I saw Faggot Kat, I could tell he'd been in a fight. I guess that man found out he was not a she!

Not long after that, I was lying up in the Courtesy Hotel with a trick, watching TV and I saw him. He was wanted for killing prostitutes. He'd been stopped and there'd been a dead body in his white van.

"Jesus!"

"That's the man I seen the other day!"

Close to death and didn't have a clue! I was glued to the TV and the next day got the paper and read more about him. He had a skin fetish. He had a thing for olive complexioned women. That baffled me. Then why was he on Terrace Ave? There are only black girls and a couple of white girls over here.

I thought that was a close encounter with death but, it was nothing compared to when my nose ring saved my life!

*The sorrows of hell compassed me about:
the snares of death prevented me. In my distress I
called upon the Lord, and cried unto my God
(Psalm 18:5-6aKJV)*

My Nose Ring

There was this girl on the stroll named Keisha*. Some people thought she looked like me. I didn't think so. She did wear her hair in finger waves same way I did. And she was shaped like me a little bit from behind but that's it. strolling, business was slow and this John and said, "Keisha?"

Well one night I was pulled up to the curve

I said, "Yeah, it's me. You want something?"

"Come take a ride with me. I've been looking for you. You haven't been around lately."

"I've been here. How you doing?"

I had already figured that Keisha knew him as a regular. So, as I'm leaning in the car, I'm looking around for his name on something so I can say it. I told him my prices. I told him where I usually go. I didn't want to go far. Don't want to be to far from the stroll, from my regulars, even though I knew they'd wait. He saw that I was hesitating. He increased the money and gave it to me upfront. That's all I needed to see. Cause it's all about the loot. I got in the car with him. We started driving up Main St. to make a left on Fulton St. I notice that he is going in the opposite direction from the Courtesy.

"Turn around. There's this spot where I usually go"

"No, I have a new spot I want to take you to"

I'm sitting back and I'm looking at him. And something about him doesn't look quite right. I'm started to get a funny feeling in the pit of my stomach.

"Where are we going? We can pull over and do it right here on the side of the road"

"No, I got this place I want to take you to."

Then we get on the parkway and he's driving faster and faster. I'm starting to get really scared because I don't know where we're going. He's not a regular and I'm just really starting to get a bad feeling in my stomach. I'm talking about anything right now, just to get his mind off of whatever he's thinking about that's making him drive so fast. Finally, for what seems like fifteen minutes or more, he pulls over. We are on the Meadowbrook Parkway parked on the grass.

"Get out", he said.

"Here?"

"Yes! I always wanted to do it in the woods. Go ahead, I have to get something."

"That's gonna cost extra."

I got out of the car. This is gonna be quick, I'm thinking. Got me all out here in the woods. He'll have to pay extra. I started walking up the side of the parkway into the woods. The moon was out and it helped me to see where I was going. I kept walking. He was behind me. He was coaxing me along and then his voice changed.

"Keisha, why did you do it?"

"Why did I do what?"

Smack! I could feel my face tingling from being slapped. He'd taken rope out of his pocket and had hit me in my face. He tied my hands behind my back. I couldn't fight back!

"You know what you did. I lost everything!"

"No tell me! What did I do?"

By then, my left eyelid was hurting and I could feel something dripping down the side of my face. I knew it was blood.

"I lost my family, my home, my career"

By then he's crying and there's something in his hand. He raised it over his head and I could see that it was an axe. I started screaming.

"My name is not Keisha! My name is April! April Cofield!"

"Your name is Keisha! And I'm going to kill you for what you did to me"

I started running, but because I was in the woods and the ground was soft I lost my shoe and then I fell. He was right behind me. He had both his hands on the axe and was holding it high over his head. I looked back at him and moved my shoulders up to try and shield my neck to prepare for the blow. I was crying. I knew I was gonna die that night. I just knew it. I was crying about my sister Karen. She was pregnant and I wouldn't live to see the baby. I couldn't move nothing but my head. I knew I was gonna die, so I moved my head up toward the sky and to the side

"Please Jesus! HELP ME!

There was silence all but my voice praying and begging God to help me.

Then...

"It's not you! You're not Keisha! Oh my God, Oh my God, OH MY GOD. What have I done? What have I done? What is that? What's that?"

"What's what?"

I rolled my shoulder up to wipe the blood and the tears. Also, thinking that I had grass on my face or something.

"What's that shining on your face?"

"What this?"

I turned my face toward the moonlight again. I knew it could only be one thing.

He shook his head, Yes!

"My nose ring. It's my nose ring. Please Mr. My name is not Keisha. Please just let me go. I won't tell nobody."

He started wailing. I mean he cried so much that I felt sorry for him. He begged me to forgive him. He looked like a wounded little boy.

"Just take me back to Terrace."

He untied my hands and we walked back to the car. He put the axe in the trunk. We got in the car and sat there for a while. The tears started flowing again. I had never been so close to death before that I could taste it. After a while I stopped crying. But I had to know.

"What did Keisha do to you so bad that you'd want to kill her?"

He waited a long time and then he told me.

"I was a regular. I was good to her. I gave her whatever she asked for. More than she charged. She became greedy. Started demanding more and more. Then she sent me pictures of us. She blackmailed me. I paid it off. But she sent the pictures to my office and to my home. My wife left me. Took my children. I lost my job. She didn't have to do that to me. Ruined my life. I lost everything! I wanted to kill her for what she did. When I saw you from behind, I thought it was her. But when the moonlight hit your nose ring; I could see your face...Please forgive me."

He started sobbing again. By this time we had been riding back, had gotten off the service road and were going back through Roosevelt, headed towards Hempstead. I looked at him. I let him take me back to Terrace and I got out of his car. I had to know how much money she got that almost cost me my life.

"How much money she get from you?"

"Ten thousand dollars."

Then I really became vexed. Got my face busted open, almost lost my life because she wouldn't do the right thing after getting 10Gs? I would've done the right thing. I would've taken care of him if he was taking care of me. He again apologized and before he left, he gave me all the money he had in his pocket. He drove off. I was still in a daze. I went and bought some weed and got high with a friend of mine. I just had to talk to somebody that night.

A couple of days later, I saw Keisha. I went up to her and bust her in the face for G.P. (general principle). But then I had to leave Hempstead. Her people were looking for me to retaliate. I still managed to service my clients by going to their places of business after hours.

He and I became friends after that. He actually became a regular customer. But then one day just like he came in my life, he left. I often wonder whatever happened to him.

I sat there looking at her. Hanging on every word that came from her mouth.

"And one other thing" she said. "From that day to this day, I never used anybody else's name and I never leave home without my nose ring!"

April and I recently drove by the spot where she almost lost her life. It was near the M7 exit on the Meadowbrook Parkway.

Short Stays

On a recent Friday afternoon, April and I drove through Hempstead heading towards Lakeview. She wanted to see the house where she and Kawand lived before the county took him into foster care. We searched but couldn't find it. I could tell she was disappointed. We left Lakeview and drove past the Courtesy Hotel. In recent months, it had been in the newspaper. The community wanted it torn down. This use to be one of her spots.

"If a trick wanted to get a room, I'd take him to one of two places. I'd either bring him here or to another spot. The Courtesy Hotel was a known spot for drug dealers and prostitutes."

She wanted me to pull in. I told her I'd prefer not to. I didn't want my car on the property. We sat at a light and stared at it. There was a sign posted over the building that said the town supervisor didn't want to help the community. The community believed that the village stopped the sale of the property. An out-of-state investor wanted to tear it down and build an upscale apartment complex on the premises. We stared at the sign. This place is a den of iniquity if there ever was one. And to think that they still have the audacity to advertise it in the Queens newspaper as though it is a wonderful spot for a romantic excursion. Don't believe the hype! Everyone in Hempstead knows that its main clients are short stays.

She had told me stories about the hotel years ago. The first account was of her in the prime of her career as a prostitute. When she looked good and took care of her body. It sounded like something you might see in a movie.

My favorite time of the year was income tax time. I pocketed many checks that were signed over and given to me for services rendered. Sometimes they'd take the time to cash them first. One time this man came on the stroll. This was early during my reign. This one trick came on the stroll one evening.

"I got one thousand dollars and nothing but time. Stay with me for the week?"

I leaned in the car and looked at him. He dropped a thousand dollars on the passenger seat to prove he was serious. And I picked

it up.

"I'll take that but then you gotta take me to the store to pick up a few things. Then I'm yours for the week."

I picked up some deodorant, some toothpaste, toothbrush, lotion, scarf for my hair and underwear. I also had him take me to the Rainbow shop to buy a couple of outfits. He got a room and we stayed there all week.

He ordered in food. We smoked weed and smoked crack. And I took care of him for the whole week. At the beginning of the seventh day when I woke up, he was gone. No falling in love. No marriage proposals. No commitments. It was always business. Always about the loot.

The second incident at the Courtesy Hotel was an account of her near the end of her career as a crack head prostitute. It sounded like something you'd see in a documentary or worse: a nightmare.

"I was there so much that I developed a relationship with the desk clerk and the maids. By now, my hygiene is terrible. I'd wear the same clothes for days on end. Thinking only of ways to get my next hit. Even when I was able to get a room, I didn't shower afterwards. I wanted to hurry and get back to the stroll. My kit no longer includes items to take care of my body. It now consists of crack paraphernalia: I have a crack pipe, lighter, 151 proof Rum, cotton and wire hangar. If a trick wanted to go there, I'd call ahead and have them give me a dirty room. That way I didn't have to pay and the trick would still give me the extra money that I required for the room."

I'm looking at my friend who over time has become my sister. I sat quietly thinking about what I just heard. I reflected back to our very first conversation when I was thinking of her as a crack head ho with a conscious. Now I'm thinking I'd like to add "scheming and nasty" to the top of the first two words and drop "with a conscious."

Decline

One day I started biting down on a sandwich and I heard a crackling sound that was coming from inside my mouth. I opened my mouth and looked down at the sandwich. It was my tooth. My tooth had cracked off and was now sticking out of the bread. I was shocked! I'd seen girls with no teeth. Never thought I'd become one of them. I thought that I could save the rest of my teeth by eating soft foods. So, I did. I ate really soft foods and if I had to bite down on something I'd push the food past my front teeth and use my tongue and the back teeth to make bite sizes. All that effort didn't change the inevitable. In a matter of weeks, I'd lost most of my teeth except the ones in the back, but it didn't stop me from eating. I always ate a little something and I never lost a lot of weight. I did lose a couple of pounds. I went down to a size fourteen, but that's it. I never lost enough weight so that people would look at me and say, "That's a crack head!"

The decline of my beauty didn't stop me from turning tricks. One day I was on the stroll. It was still early in the day and there were a few kids hanging out. This young girl approached me, looked at me and called me a crack head prostitute. At first, it startled me, then I started to curse her out. I just knew she wasn't talking about me. A couple of days went by and I was walking past a parked car. An unfamiliar face caught my attention. It was a crack head prostitute. She had a nose ring on like mine. She moved her hand up to touch her face just like I did. I stopped and looked closer. It was my reflection on the car's window. That crack head prostitute was me.

I Want You

There are many testimonies of how people came to Christ. There are those who claim to have heard his voice. Some felt His presence. And others simply got to a point where they realized that enough is enough. April's encounter with Christ was not like the life she lived. He'd made several attempts to reach her. She admitted to using jail as the only time that she stepped foot in a church. She was in jail quite a bit. She told us of all the times that others prayed for her. In the midst of her trials, he'd dispensed angels around her. She'd even shared how the moon that shone brightly that fateful evening and illumined her nose ring, saved her life. He'd been trying for a long time to reach her. This time he'd speak directly to her soul. I want you!

In Ecclesiastes chapter 3 the bible declares that: **To everything there is a season, and a time to every purpose under the heaven: A time to plant and a time to pluck that which is planted. A time to keep silence and a time to speak. A time to break down and a time to build up. And a time to be born and a time to die (KJV).**

After eight years and all that she's told me, I know that the account of her life on the street could go on and on but even I, as a witness, have grown weary for her. I'm convinced that there comes a point in our lives that we must be silent so that we can hear. She was. He spoke. If we are merely existing and not living a purposeful life according to God's will, then we must be torn down. Some of us must experience this again and again. She did; multiple times. The bible tells us that He loves us and cares enough that He knows the number of hairs on our head. He knew hers. He knew that her life still held purpose and could be used for goodness. He would build her up. But to do this, there must be a death; so that there could be a resurrection. She must die, so that He can live!

Knowing this, that our old man (woman) is crucified with Him. That the body of sin might be destroyed, that henceforth we should not serve sin. For he that is dead is freed from sin.
(Romans 6:6-7KJV)

The Death of April Cofield
February 16, 1995

There are many dates that will stay with me for the rest of my life. My birthday, the birthdays of my children and my grandchild. Most recovering addicts can tell you the date, down to months, days and minutes since they've been drug free. There is another date that will always be with me.

February 16,1995. Mineola Vice was doing a sting operation. They were arresting everybody on the street. They picked me up and took me down to the Mineola Precinct. They took me to an office and cuffed me to a desk. They started interrogating me. "Ms. Cofield, listen. Let us know what's going on over there."

"What you mean what's going on? You know what's going on over there!"

"You don't even have to be here right now. We want to let you go just give us that cat's name you were talking to."

They were baiting me. I knew what they were talking about. I recalled a conversation that I had a couple of days earlier. I knew this man who was a drug dealer. He had just come home from upstate and he came up to me while I was strolling.

"Ms. Cofield not only do I have the best crack but I have guns, too."

I didn't want a gun.

"Naah! No guns, partner but, I'll take a couple of them rocks." We took care of the business and I was on my way.

"Well Ima still get back with you."

I thought about him. I gave them his name and told them what happened. They let me sit down and I started writing out the statement. Suddenly, I heard a voice say,

"Just go ahead and do it."

I looked around to see who was talking to me. I was doing it. I was almost finished writing the statement!

"Do what?"

The police officers were looking at me. They thought I was high but, I wasn't.

"Just go ahead and do it."

"Ms. Cofield, is everything all right? Just sign here. Right here and you're free to go!"

That's what the officers said to me. I looked at the statement. The voice was still going through my body, reaching down into my soul and I could still hear it,

"Just go ahead and do it"

This time I recognized the voice. And this time I would obey it! I tore up the statement. The detectives went crazy! You would've thought that I was ripping up money. They started scrambling for the ripped up papers. They stared at me in disbelief. They could not believe that I would choose jail time instead of signing the statement. A couple of them started yelling and cursing at me. I simply leaned back in the chair. One officer stood and came over to me with handcuffs.

"April Cofield, you're under arrest. You have the right to remain silent or anything that you say will be used against you in a court of law. You have the right to an attorney..."

He uncuffed me from the table, stood me up and cuffed my hands behind my back. He started reading me my rights. Then suddenly, I started feeling a tingling sensation that started from the top of my head and ran through my body. I had never experienced anything like that in my whole life! I felt that a huge burden was lifted off my shoulders.

On my way to jail, nothing was the same. Not the ride in the police car. Not the way they cuffed me. I felt like weights were dropping off me. I got my one phone call and I called my Aunt Bobbie. She was gonna pay the fine. But I told her:

"No, I have to go ahead and do this"

"Well, I'll be praying for you." she told me.

It took about four hours to process me back into the system. Then I spent seventy-two hours in new admit. I thought I was going to the DART dorm after that. I didn't. They put me in C dorm. I walked into the cell and dropped to my knees and I said,

"Please forgive me. Please forgive me."

Therefore we are buried with him by baptism into death: that like as Christ was raised up from the dead by the glory of the Father, even so we also should walk in newness of life. (Romans 6:4 KJV)

Rebirth of the Spiritual Woman

I was assigned to the regular dorms. I didn't go into D.A.R.T. this time. I was there so much that it felt like the red carpet was always rolled out for me. Not this time. I didn't want the notoriety that I'd had before. I was a different person. I knew it. I knew that this was my last bid. One night I felt an overwhelming desire to tell God that I would spend the rest of my life serving Him. I wanted Him to know that I'd spent many years working in Satan's kingdom, and that I now wanted to devote my life to Him in service. In my dorm on Cell Block D 3 C 21, I made a vow that I would do anything he asked me to do:

"Whatever you tell me to do, Lord I'll do it. Whatever you ask me to do, Lord, I'll do it."

I remember crying out and thanking him for saving me.

Hi, my name is April Cofield. Does anybody wanna pray with me? I would stand in the middle of the dorm and ask the same question every day. No one would answer. They would just look at me like I had five heads. Some of them even mocked me saying,

"Ms. Cofield you know you going back out there and smoke crack. You ain't changed."

There were times before that what they said would've been true. This time was different. I would go to my cell and sit alone and pray or read the bible. After asking several days, one person came forth and said, I'll pray with you, April. She came and then soon there were others.

There was this one woman who had been watching me pray with the small group of women. She never came over to join us, but she'd just watch from a distance. One day she came up to me and started talking about this therapeutic community. She called it TOPIC House. Treatment of People in Crisis. I wanted to know everything about it. She told me all that she could remember and gave me a name. I wanted to know how I could get in there. I'm thinking if I can get to that place, I won't be homeless or hungry anymore. I didn't understand therapeutic community. I just thought that I wanted to be there. She gave me the address and I wrote them.

One day I had a visit. I had forgotten how much of a hassle it was to prepare for a visit. I didn't even know who it was. I got down to the visitor's room and it was a man. I didn't recognize him. I hadn't asked to speak to a lawyer or anything so I couldn't imagine who it was. I sat down across the table in front of him.

"Hello April, my name is Michael* and I'm here from TOPIC House. We received your letter and are interested in having you become a client in our community. So, I need to take down some information about you"

He took down personal information then he started asking questions. Then he started asking me general questions. "Why do you want to come to TOPIC House?"

"God has me on a new journey. My life is changing. I asked God why should I go there? So I guess it must be something that I need to learn, grow or die to self. I don't know. I just don't wanna be broke and homeless anymore and I wanna live a righteous life.

A better life. I know with God in my heart and with Jesus in my life, I will go all out."

He looked surprised.

"You have such determination. I interview thousands of people. Some tell me what they think I want to hear just so they can get out of jail."

"I am feeling grateful right now because I had never made a decision to change but this time it's different."

He thanked me for my time and I thanked him and I went back upstairs. Afterwards, I was so excited. My sisters started encouraging me. The following week he came back and told me that I was accepted into the program. I was so overjoyed. He told me more about the program and then he said that he would be there to pick me up when I was released and take me to TOPIC house. Those last couple of weeks in jail, I was a model inmate. I wasn't going to let anything stop me from starting this next phase of my life.

But he knoweth the way that I take:
when he hath tried me,
I shall come forth as pure gold.
(Job 23:10 KJV)

No Testimony Without a Test

My release date was on a Friday. I walked through the gates but, I didn't see him. I stood out there. Before, I would walk up to Carman Ave. hoping to get a trick. This time I'd made a promise and I knew that I'd keep it. I stood there for 45 minutes. He hadn't come. A cab pulled up. And someone I knew hopped out. We greeted each other. She was coming to visit someone there. Ms. Cofield, I know it's been a long time, so I got some weed. Cigarettes. You want something. No, I'm on my way. Well you take care of yourself. The cab drivers waiting there.

"Well are you getting in?"

I really had no intention of it, but I said yes.

"Where you going, Terrace Ave?"

"Okay, I'll let you off on the Bedell side"

"No. Let me off at the middle section." On the ride there, he kept watching me.

"So where you going?"

"I was waiting for someone to pick me up. I am going to TOPIC house."

He stopped in the middle section of Terrace and I paid the fare. I walked into the building and went to my Aunt Bobbie's house. I looked at her and walked into her outstretched arms. I started crying.

"He wasn't there to get me to take me to TOPIC house."

"Niece, the devil is a liar. You are going to TOPIC house. Do you have a number?"

I did. I had it written down on a piece of paper. My aunt called them.

"My name is Bobbie and my niece was to start the program today. She's here. The person that was supposed to pick her up didn't." She listened to the person on the phone as I anxiously stood by.

"Monday? You'll hold her bed for her until Monday?" They must've said yes.

"Thank you. My niece will be there."

She hung up the phone.

"Didn't I tell you the devil's a liar?"

She grabbed my hands and prayed with me that God would protect me and that His will be done in me and that I rebuke the devil in Jesus name. I wiped my tears.

"Niece are you hungry? I don't have a whole lot of money." She pulled out a fifty dollar bill.

"Go get something to eat and come off your fast. I will send you there in a cab. What's the address?"

They told her. I left her apartment and walked down Terrace and realized that I was on the same route like I was on the stroll. But I was dressed differently. I started singing, He's sweet I know. I was walking up North Franklin near State Farm Insurance.

"Psst. Psst."

There was a voice coming out of the alley way that was beside the theater.

"How you doing, April?"

"I'm blessed."

He pulled out two twenties. I knew what he wanted. I put my hand on his.

"I don't live like that no more. I'm a new creature."

"You do look different."

"Well, God bless you"

And I walked off. Then I heard a car pulling up behind me. It was a familiar car. It was one of my base dates. He stopped and I got in the car. He put five one hundred dollar bills in my hand. I looked at it.

"I heard you were coming home. Some of the ladies told me you got out today."

"The devil is a liar."

"What did you say?"

"I said the devil is liar and I'm a new creature in Christ." He sighed.

"Okay, if you won't go out with me can you at least get me some drugs?"

"No, I can't do that but I'll be praying for you."

I gave him back the five hundred dollars. I got out of the car.

"Thank you Jesus. No weapon formed against me will prosper!" I knew at that moment that I was being tested. I walked into the Chinese food store and ordered my food. After it was ready, I paid for it and left. I didn't want to go the same way that I'd come, so I walked up the Jackson Ave. side. I turned onto Terrace and I saw some drug dealers that I once dealt with. They were happy to see me. Not only was I one of their best customers but I would purchase for my tricks and refer other customers to them. They had also heard that I had taken a bid rather than tell what I knew. In other words, I had earned their utmost respect. I wanted to walk past them but the Holy Spirit compelled me to go in and talk to all of them. They knew I'd been in jail and thought I wanted a hit. This one crack head came up to me with some crack.

"We got something for you. We got the bells. We gonna get you on your feet."

"I don't live like this no more. God loves you and you don't have to live like this anymore, either. We don't have to be stuck anymore."

I looked at them and they looked at me and I walked out because at that point, I knew that I had been tested again. Three times in short of an hour. Three times! I got to my Aunt's house and told her what happened. She knew my struggles. She'd seen me on the street selling my body and she'd visited me and sent me money while I was in jail. This might've seemed small to most people but my aunt and I knew that this was worthy of praise! We ate and talked until it was time for me to leave.

"Do you have any clothes to take to TOPIC House?"

I thought about it for a minute. I had the clothes on my back. I'm sure she probably had a couple of things that I could wear. Then I remembered I had some clothes that I kept in a crack den down the hall. I started hoping that she wasn't thinking about those things. I was wrong.

"You need to go get your things, April."

"I don't wanna go there. I don't want those things!"

"April, go there anyway. You might find some things you can use."

I left her apartment and went to the crack den to get my stuff. I knocked on the door and no one answered. I knew it wasn't locked. It never was. I walked in and there was no one there. I felt overjoyed about that. I guess God said, three tests in one day is enough for anybody. Let me not push it! I walked inside and there was my stuff in a big black garbage bag. I dragged it out into the hallway and down to my aunt's apartment. I didn't want to bring it inside. I knew there were some seedy clothes in the bag but I was afraid of what might crawl out, also. So, I started going through it in the hallway. I found crack pipes with residue in it and other crack paraphernalia. I grabbed some things that I could use and threw the rest of it in the garbage dumpster. My aunt called me a cab. I thanked her for everything that she had done for me. She walked me to the middle of the block to wait for the cab. I saw my Goddaughter. She looked at me and noticed the bags in my hand.

"What you doing God mommy? You doing your thing this time?"
"I'm doing it, sweetheart. I'm on my way, God Child. I love you and I'm praying for your soul and thanking God for your deliverance right now!"

I spoke that thing as though it is!

"Alright God mommy gotta go."

She had a couple of drug dealers waiting for her to deliver some packages. As she approached them I could hear them say:

"Where is April, going?"

She looked back at me and responded.

"She's on a different journey now."

Finally the cab pulled up in front of the building. I gave him the address and he told me the fare. There was still enough money left over from the money my Aunt had given me to cover the fare. I got in the cab, hugged my aunt good bye and left Terrace Ave. on my way to Topic House.

TOPIC House

June 16, 2007 When April first told me about TOPIC House, I'd imagined a small wooden framed house. I would always imagine that it had lots of windows so that the sun's rays could gently caress the faces of the residents waking them up without the sound of an alarm. In my mind, there were ten residents who all needed a haven to escape their past lives. I was wrong in my assumption. It was a beautiful Saturday morning when we pulled up in front of an unoccupied brick mansion. Although the grass on the premises needed cutting and the building was in need of minor repairs, I could see the original grandeur spring forth and all the memories from April's journals came to life.

I parked the car in the lot and turned off the engine. April got out of the car and walked around to the front door and checked. It was locked. She walked around to the right side and stepped up onto a veranda. She peered in the window.

"Come and look, Robin."

I was hesitant. I wanted this to be her moment. This was to be her time to recollect. I just wanted to witness it safely from my car. Not that I was afraid. I wasn't. Its just that the memory of Terrace and Bedell was still so raw and fresh in my mind that I could still feel eyes that bored through the back of my head as I dared make eye contact. You have to see but not see. Hear but feign deafness. I didn't

The know how to do that. April taught me. The last time we were there, I wanted to run like h--- but she looked at me and said,

"I know what you're thinking. Don't do it!"

I knew then from the tone of her voice to do as she said. That same tone was present on that Saturday morning. She wanted me *to be in the moment with her, so reluctantly; I got out of the car. Growing up in the south, you know not to step on anyone's property without permission. I felt uneasy but, I was with April. mega strength!*

TOPIC house was a residential treatment center with a men's wing and a women's wing. They prepared the residents to reenter society. The counseling sessions addressed addiction and health issues. They supported the residents with educational opportunities and career training. Some of the residents were mandated there for treatment. April was there voluntarily. Some of the residents stayed for six months. April stayed for two years.

We stood there. April looked in the window at the grand ballroom. She was probably reminiscing about her graduation. I watched her; taking in her excitement of finally sharing this place with me.

"Being at TOPIC House was the hardest thing I've ever done in my life. I'd rather have two more babies than go back through TOPIC house."

"Why?"

Because you're forced to face the one person you've avoided probably most of your life: Yourself!

My First Day

The ride there was so amazing! I felt like I was going to another world. It was about a half hour. I opened my bible and turned to Matthew 6:25. I started praising God and I know the cab driver thought that I was crazy but as we drove and he watched from the rearview mirror, he never said it. We got off the main road and passed by big buildings and went up a hill. I could sense that we were almost there. I started praying,

"Whatever it is that you would have me do, Lord. Make my spirit willing to do it according to your will and purpose for my life."

The cabdriver pulled up in front of the building. I paid him and got out of the cab with my bags. I walked up the steps to the front door and looked down. "Welcome" was the word written on the mat at the front door. Once I walked in another mat said: Change is Pain. I went in and gave them my name. The coordinator on duty came down. The house was put on "total band" which means that no one could talk to or make contact with anyone except the coordinator. The coordinator came over to talk with me. She started explaining the program. There were four phases in TOPIC house. As a newbie, I was in Phase I. I must've had a look on my face. "Don't be nervous." She said.

All new comers were screened. After my screening, my bags were searched for contraband. While all this was going on, ! was put in the Contemplation room. News of my arrival spread quickly and the women started breaking band. There were so many people breaking band that they stopped the screening and escorted me to the office.

"There are four women who are saying that they don't wanna be on the wing with you", the coordinator said. "They want to be on total band with you."

"Well I can understand why they feel that way. They don't know that I've changed. The old April; they need to be afraid of her. But I am a new creature and they don't need to be afraid of me."

They put me back in the screening room and continued the process. They gave me a mentor who became known as my big sister. Her name was Gerry*. Gerry took me on a tour enroute to the wing where the women dormed. I would be sharing a room with Gerry. We went in and I stood there for a moment. It had bunk beds in it and sorta reminded me of being in jail at first. But I knew that it wasn't because I could see the trees, hear the birds, and most of all, there were no bars. Even though I usually don't like change, this was a new experience for me and it felt good. It felt right. Some people may wonder how can this be? How could I like being in a place that sounded a lot like jail? This was different and I knew it. All I'd known for many years was going to jail and surviving on Terrace. Surviving on Terrace and going to jail. I started crying.

"Why are you crying?"

"Because, I'm so blessed."

She started crying with me.

"April, I hope you stay here because this place could use a person like you."

"A person like Me?"

She didn't answer. She just showed me my room and helped me make up my bed. Women who didn't know me and those that did started coming in and giving me things that they knew I needed. I was so grateful that God did that for me. Gerry told me that I had to be with her where ever she went because I didn't have strength.

"How do I get strength?"

"The longer you stay here, the stronger you'll get."

I knew that I would get stronger because I wasn't going anywhere. I was gonna stay there because I didn't have anywhere else to go. I realized that this was gonna be another part of my journey but I didn't realize how hard it was gonna be. I knew that whatever it was God would bring me through.

Privileges are given out in four phases. Phase I requires you to run a morning meeting. After that you can get a radio for your room, then receive letters and phone calls.

On my second day, I experienced a full range of emotions. I had never been in a therapeutic community unless you count my years in jail. I looked around the room and saw a sign that read: God have mercy on TOPIC House. I was praying that He would and I'd be included. The day was structured in very much the same manner as a prison. You were told when to eat. You were told when to meet with this group or that group. My big sister gave me more rules on what to expect and to memorize. It was so much to remember that I started my first journal. Time went on and Phase 1 became Phase 2 rather quickly. In the process of going from one meeting to another, sixty days had passed.

One of the most important things that I found out was that I would be able to see a medical doctor, a dentist and speak to counselors as well. God knew that I was in desperate need of health care.

A Woman's Smile

April has a beautiful smile. But I know that it wasn't always beautiful. We know how she lost her teeth therefore; the restoration of her smile is also a part of the puzzle.

April always had pain in her teeth and once she lost them, pain in her gums. The pain was hardly noticeable when she was high. But her teeth were very sensitive and the pain sometimes excruciating when she was clean and sober. The only dental work she ever received was when she was incarcerated.

I was escorting another sister resident to social services and saw a good friend of mine. She hugged me and said, "April, make sure you get you some teeth while you at TOPIC House." I loved her boldness, how she just came out with the truth. I was conscious of my teeth. It stopped me from smiling but it didn't bother me enough that I was gonna stop talking. I thought about what she said. The next day, I approached my counselor and asked him about me getting some teeth.

"It has come up in our staff meetings, April. We are aware that you need help. It'll take ninety days for your Medicaid to kick in. I'll put in the request for you."

He went before the board with my request. All decisions regarding clients were discussed and decided on in the privilege meeting.

He went to the meeting and presented my case. They all agreed unanimously that I could have the oral surgery.

The dentist looked in my mouth and I could tell by the look he gave me, it wasn't good.

"What happened to you, April?"

"I'm a recovering addict"

"I understand that but, drugs wouldn't do this."

"Who did this to you? Who broke off the teeth in your mouth?" I didn't answer him. I honestly didn't know what he meant. I guess, though, it had to be the dentist in jail or the crack that I smoked.

"You will need major oral surgery. I will have to get permission to do this surgery because you'll need general anesthesia."

He moved the tools and started writing down notes. I wiped my mouth and thanked him. I got up from the chair and left. I arrived back at TOPIC House and I told my counselor what the doctor said. He said he'd wait to get the paperwork from the dentist. Once he received them, he wrote up an order requesting the surgery. I received clearance to have oral surgery. The surgeon removed the remaining nubs and roots that were left in my gums. He also measured me for dentures. He told me to smile.

"You have a nice smile, April."

I looked in the mirror. All I could see was that my mouth was folded in and I could barely see my lips. How could he look at me in this condition and see that I had a beautiful smile?

I had the surgery. I had to be on bed rest for a while. I had gauze in my mouth and was on antibiotics. It took a while to heal. I had to eat very soft foods. Then once I healed I went back to the dentist and they put putty in my mouth to make the mold for my teeth. About a month and a half later, my teeth were ready. I was nervous and excited. I had forgotten what I looked like with teeth in my mouth. I went to the dentist's office. He took the teeth out of plastic container. They looked like they belong to someone else. He helped me put them in. They felt funny. The doctor asked me to look in the mirror. I stood there and looked at the person in the mirror. Wow! It was not that of a crack head prostitute. I saw a woman in the mirror and she had a beautiful smile.

High Risk Category

I had to do a physical once I entered TOPIC House. I've always felt uneasy about going to doctors, especially because of my history. I filled out the health information forms and gave them to the nurse. The nurse asked me questions about my health.

"Have you taken an HIV test?"

"Yes. I took them each time I went to jail."

"Do you know the results?"

"I started getting tested in 1991, but I never knew the results."

When you are a known prostitute in Hempstead that was one of the requirements before you were sentenced. The judge had to know the health status of all known prostitutes both male and female. I started thinking about her question and I remembered something from my past.

I know that I slept with a person that was HIV positive. I met him on the stroll. It was early morning and he was in the beginning of his recovery. He told me that he had admired me and he wanted to be with me.

"Hello Ms."

He was a good looking brother.

"No offense, but I don't deal with black men."

"I understand that."

By the way he answered, I could tell that he knew that about me. He was a nice looking man.

"Do you carry condoms?"

"Sometimes. Not all the time."

"You should carry them all the time."

"Well, I don't. It's about the loot for me. I got to get the money."

He understood that.

"But look here. No matter what you do, don't ever do a "BJ" without a condom."

I didn't particularly like that, but I appreciated the concern.

"Why are you talking to me like that? How much money do you have?"

"Why don't I take you to the hotel. I got a hundred dollars."

He knew I needed a hit.

"I guess you want to stop and get your stuff?"

"I guess I better do that because you talking about spending the day."

I was glad about it because I needed a break. I had been strolling all night. I wasn't concerned about the casualties. You know, whether he had a wife or girlfriend. Anyway, I took him to the hotel and he got the room. He had a lot of condoms. I asked him,

"Why you got all those condoms? You don't have a girlfriend or wife?"

"No, I just need to be on the safe side."

"Why is that?"

"I just need to be on the safe side. You want to take your hit?"

"No, I just want to do this, then I'll take my hit."

So we had foreplay. Something that I don't usually like to do, but I did. A part of me at that moment felt like, let me just relax. Not take him from the trick category, but let me relax enough to just be with this person. I didn't quite look at him like a trick. He was a trick, because he was paying me but he wasn't because he appeared to be concerned about me. So I did him. I became slightly interested. We had a good conversation.

"You are a beautiful woman you don't need to be on the street."

"I appreciate your concern."

I let down my battle armor of do and go, do and go. So I stayed with him and we just talked. He gave me another fifty dollars. We were enjoying each other's company and then he asked me,

"You hungry?"

"Not really. Just want something to drink."

So he gave me the money for that. I slipped on my jacket and my heels. I put the money in my shoe. No way was I leaving my loot in the room. I went downstairs, and there was a soda machine in the lobby. There was a woman down stairs and there was this chick downstairs staring at me. I went back upstairs. Before he left, he said,

"You don't know who is HIV positive."

"Are you HIV positive?"

"I am. That's why I didn't want you to give me a blow job."

"Well I appreciate you caring enough to tell me and for not asking me to do that for you. But I did kiss you."

"You can't get HIV from kissing. I'll see you around and be careful out there."

He left. I couldn't wait for him to leave after that. I wanted a hit, but I also wanted to shower. I was dressed kind of fancy for a Sunday afternoon and I knew that I needed to catch a cab back to Terrace or walk, but if I did, I knew that I'd get a date.

It wasn't until I got in TOPIC House that I thought about him. The nurse continued, "It's good to follow your status because you are high risk."

She tested me and told me that I couldn't have sex for ninety days. I couldn't anyway, because I was in TOPIC House. Thirty days went by and the nurses called me in the office.

"I got your test results, April."

"Okay"

I held my breath.

"You're HIV negative."

I started crying. She started comforting me.

"You want to keep getting tested because the disease can lay dormant for ten years."

"I will"

I started getting tested every six months. I know that only God could do this for me and I don't take it lightly. I've lost a lot of friends to the "Monster." That's what we called it on the streets. It's almost like you'd rather hear that they got shot or murdered than to hear that they died from the monster. But I know it's only by the grace of God that I am HIV negative and for that I am thankful.

More Memories of TOPIC House

I use to think that God brought me to TOPIC house so that I wouldn't be broke and homeless. I realize that I was brought there for so much more. I was the only person there who wasn't mandated to be there. It surprised everyone that I stayed and endured that time. I believe that I was mandated by God. I never graduated from high school so the first thing on my list was getting my GED. The teacher came twice a week. Her name was Ms. Gladys*. She taught the adult GED program. She was a very compassionate woman. She would explain English so well that even a baby would've understood.

Ms. Gladys gave us the practice GED test. It didn't discourage me as it did most people. I had to wait a couple of days to get the results of the test. 210 is the passing score. I got a 204 on the test. Paul, the educational counselor, told me that I should take the test again. I will do just that.

Ms. Gladys had promised me she'd take me with her to church. I was excited about going. First, because as I said, I'd always felt like Ms. Gladys was an angel. I knew if this was the church that she chose to go to then it must be alright for me. She picked me up and we pulled up in front of the church on Babylon Tpke. with the big steps. The steps weren't so big, they were just steep and there were a lot of them. I knew this church very well. I use to stroll right down the street from this church. I also played handball in Centennial Park which is right down the street. I knew it was there but, I'd never gone in before.

The visitors were asked to stand up. I did and introduced myself. Some of the people seemed to recognize my name. I remembered that I had asked Ms. Gladys to pray for me. She did and had written my name on a prayer card, so the entire church had been praying for me as well. That's why I am vigilant about sending up prayer cards. People that didn't know me had been praying for me. It's true that prayer changes things!

I went in and the spirit was so high in that place that I could hardly sit in my seat. The pastor and the elders stood in the front and asked if there was anyone who wanted to develop a relationship with Jesus Christ. I stood up and it took everything in me not to run down that aisle towards the front of the church. I already knew that I belonged to God. I just needed a place filled with others who felt the same way. That was my first visit to my future church home.

Phase 3 is a transitional phase when you are working and actively seeking to find a place to live, preparation for reentering society. My first job was at the Plainview hotel. I had to take it because I couldn't find one in my field as a home health aide. No one would hire me. After some time, I was allowed to work offsite. I was trained in the medical field as a nurse's assistant, but because I didn't have my GED I couldn't work in that field. I took the only job I could get. I became a maid in the Plainview Plaza Hotel. My first day of work was difficult. I tell you. I had to swallow my pride. I had taken tricks into a lot of hotels but I had never had to clean one. Every day that I was there was difficult because I knew the guests that were prostitutes and tricks. A prostitute can always spot another prostitute and I surely can spot a trick when I see one. I wonder if any of them had the hookup like I had? Calling ahead to make a reservation for a dirty room. I cringe at the thought as I clean up behind some of those "business" meetings. I cringe realizing that at one time, that was my life. That was me.

I worked at the hotel from eight to five. I'd call TOPIC House and have someone save me a plate of food. I worked at the hotel for one year.

My time at TOPIC House was coming to an end. I had a job and had become a responsible person. I felt truly blessed. I knew if I could complete two years of therapy at TOPIC House then I could do anything through Christ who gives me strength. I knew that I would be graduating soon so I started preparing for reentry into society. I had saved my money from working at the hotel. I had no bills or expenses. I had a place to sleep. I had food. So all of my wages went into a T-stage account so that I could have money saved when I re-entered society.

I contacted a realtor. I knew that I needed a safe place to stay. I couldn't go home and I couldn't go back to the streets. I had to go someplace drug free and far away from the temptations. One of my house mates, Sasha and I decided that since we were roommates for so long that we would room together on the outside. We started looking for an apartment together. I started noticing the signs that were oh so familiar. She started back getting high again. I knew I didn't need to be near that temptation. I called the realtor back and told her the situation. I knew that I couldn't afford an apartment by myself so I decided that I wanted to get a room. I went back to my case worker and I told him. He understood and felt that it was fine. He told Sasha what I'd said and she stepped to me.

"Why did you do that April. I thought that real people do real things?"

"They do! But to thy own self be true."

I knew in my heart that it wouldn't work because my journey was different from hers and I didn't want to be with a roommate that might hinder my journey. I felt bad that she felt that way, but because of Jesus, I was humble and I was able to explain it to her.

"My journey is spiritual."

We talked it through, cried and ended in a good place. We are still friends to this day. I went back to the realtor. I told my testimony. I told her everything. She stopped me and said;

"I have the perfect place for you."

She took me to a spot in Uniondale. We entered a ground level apartment on Waldorf Place. I went in and immediately fell in love with it. I knew that I was home. It was $129.00 a week for rent. I had to give two months rent and one month security. I gave them the money and went back to my counselor and told him about the place. Even though I had already found the place and put money down on it, the staff at TOPIC House had to meet to decide if I was ready to reenter society. I knew I was and they voted on it. They all voted yes! After two years they knew that I was ready. I walked up and down that wing, praising God! I had mixed emotions. I was excited, but also sad because I had gotten used to living with them. I packed my things and began phase 4.

Phase 4 is the reentry phase when you are out in the community working and living. You still report back to TOPIC House for ninety days for urine tests and have counseling until you have graduated.

It was moving day. I had all my things and I had my key. I went into the apartment. I stepped through the door and I just cried. I knew that only God could do this for me. Only Him! That night it was very quiet. No quieter than usual, I guess. It's just that quietness in a facility or therapeutic community is not the same as quiet in a home. It was deafening. I couldn't take it, so I went outside about 10PM to see the stars. I just started talking and praying to God.

"I can't do this without you and I need you. I don't know my destiny but I know I'm in the palm of your hands and I just want your will to be done, Lord."

I went back in and had the most peaceful rest that I'd had in some time.

I was adjusting to life on the outside very well, but there were still some rules that I had to abide by until I had finished my ninety days probation. There was a rule that you can't get involved with anyone in the house, even while you are outside during your 90 day period.

I was doing so well until I started experiencing spiritual warfare. My fleshly needs started kicking in and I got involved with a fellow brother resident who was getting weekends to leave the house. We were not supposed to fraternize with each other while we were at TOPIC house or while we were reentering society. I shouldn't have, but I did. He told somebody and that person dropped guilt. That's when you tell something you know. By now, I was well into my probationary period and only had about thirty days left. The staff called me in.

"April, were you involved with a fellow resident?" "No"

"I got too many people telling me that you were!"

I lied again.

"No!"

I was angry. But even more so, I was upset that I'd disappointed them. They called me their poster child. I had been there longer than anyone else. I had worked my way up the ranks and was now so close to graduating that it was unbelievable that I did that! But I'm a woman with needs. One part of me wanted to quit. So what, I wouldn't get what I'd worked so hard to attain. A lot of folks left TOPIC house without graduating. I struggled with it for two weeks. One day a peace came over me. I knew that I couldn't quit and I knew that I had to do what had always been hard for me to do and that was accept responsibility. As much as I disagreed with that rule, it was still one that I had to obey. So I went back to TOPIC House and said:

"I admit, I did it and I'm sorry! I'm ready to start my T stage over."

I was reprimanded back to 90 days, which meant that I had to report to them another 90 more days. I understood why I had to do this right. There were so many looking up to me as their example. With God's help, I made it through the next 90 days. The day that I'd been praying for finally came. Some of the members of my family came. A lot of the residents were introducing their relatives to me. I cried tears of joy the day that I walked across the floor in the main meeting room to receive my certificate. They awarded me the topic house medallion. On the back of the medallion was written: "Don't Quit."

Ms. Gladys walked in with a big bouquet of flowers. We were both crying tears of joy. I have to honestly say that this woman had an impact on my life. Some call it tough love. For some of us that's all we know. But for me, the counseling at TOPIC House, my renewed self-esteem and my relationship with my Lord and Savior, Jesus Christ, helped save my life. I was there to learn to make better choices and right decisions. I needed to learn to be responsible and to work on my presentation skills. My presentation skills were funky at one time. And God needed to fix that so that I could work for Him.

I don't take it lightly that I am blessed to have only experienced going in a therapeutic community once. There are people called "TCBs", which means therapeutic community bums. They are usually not successful, because they do it for the wrong reason. I didn't do this for my family, or anyone else; I did this for me. I knew that I would be dead if I didn't go there. Going to TOPIC House was one of the greatest experiences of my life. I thank God in the name of Jesus that I am no longer in a crisis, but am recovering one day at a time.

Six dollars and a Dream

After leaving the TOPIC House I had to find a job closer to home. I had been looking for a while but I finally landed a part time job. I started working as a home health care attendant to an elderly lady in Roosevelt. No one wanted Mother Clark as a patient. She had approximately thirty or forty cats. The house smelled really bad and it reeked with urine. I needed a job and after being in crack dens and working as a maid at a hotel, I knew that I could do it.

I soon understood why it was hard to place a home health care worker in that position. It was my job to take care of her but before I could that, I had to clean up after the cats. The whole house smelled and I use to cry while cleaning the house because it was such a mess. I knew that God had a plan but I didn't understand His will regarding this situation. In time, I would.

I worked two days a week. I finally received my first check. I couldn't wait to open it. I looked at the check and saw that my take home pay was $135.00 a week. My rent was a $129.00 a week. I started doing the math in my head. That meant that I was only left with six dollars to live on. The bus ride to my job was $3.00 roundtrip. I couldn't afford to take the bus. I tried to save the six dollars each week so that I could get groceries but it was nearly impossible. I purchased pancake batter and syrup. I ate pancakes everyday. When I didn't want that, I could always get on the bus and go to TOPIC House to eat. The sign at the door was still there. Welcome.

The end of the year came and I filed my taxes. I got a refund of six hundred dollars. I took a portion of that money and tithed it at a church that I visited. I took some of it and purchased a bike and I saved the rest. I was excited and afraid. It was the first time that I'd made a major purchase. I would ride the bike everywhere I went. To work, to church, everywhere.

I continued working with Mother Clarke. They needed me to do more hours so, my hours increased from part time to full time. I started working eight hours a day, seven days a week. I was now making $325.00 a week. Even in that situation, with all the smells and the cats, God blessed me.

Good News in The Mail

March 6- I took off from work. I had an appointment with my therapist. It had rained that day. The mailman had dropped off the mail and by the time I got home, the mail was wet. It was a letter from the GED program. I thought it was just another letter stating that I had failed again after my third try. I took the mail inside and opened it. Inside was a diploma stating that I had passed the test for the General Equivalency Diploma Exam. I was so filled with joy that I dropped to my knees and started praising God. When I finished praising Him and thanking Him, I called the person that supported me through the whole process: Ms. Gladys.

*Who art thou, Lord? And the Lord said, I am
Jesus, whom thou persecutest: it is hard for thee to
kick against the pricks. And he trembling and
astonished said, Lord, what wilt thou have me to
do? And the Lord said unto him, Arise, and go
into the city, and it shall be told thee what thou
must do. (Acts 9:5-6 KJV)*

The Call

One day I had gotten home after work and was checking my phone messages. The message was, "Hey girl. You know who this is. Give me a call." I knew immediately who it was. It was a fellow inmate that I had dormed with during one of my incarcerations. I was upset that she'd called me because she had given me a hard time and talked about me. I didn't return the call. A couple of days later my phone rang and I answered it. It was her. I didn't want to talk to her but decided to.

"I wanna know what you doing on Mondays?"

"Why?"

"Cause I do a meeting in the DART dorm on Mondays and I want you to speak for me."

"Yes, I'll go."

"Alright, but you can't go in there and talk about Jesus, though."

Then I got mad. How can I share my experience, strength and hope? How can I share my testimony without talking about Jesus? I was silent.

"You there?"

"First of all, I can't tell my story without talking about my Lord and Savior Jesus Christ. In order for me to recover, I had to be delivered!"

"Yeah. Yeah. Yeah. Yeah. Do you wanna come in the dorm or not?"

"No! Not, if I can't talk about Jesus!"

I hung up the phone. I was vexed for a while.

I realized that in order for me to keep what I got, I had to give it away. I also had to stop looking at the messenger and listen to the message.

One night I was home alone and I heard God's voice. He told me that I must go back into prison to give hope and teach the ones that are left behind about Jesus Christ. My response was clear, "Not me, Lord! I'm not going back in there. Why would you send me back there? Why me? Why me? Lord Jesus, ask me to do anything else but this, Lord. Please remove this from me. I don't want to go back into that place. I'm free!" I had an attitude with him! I really did. I had a pity party like you wouldn't believe! Feeling sorry for myself. Then it was revealed to me that when I was kneeling down on that cement floor in Cell Block D 3 C 21 that I made a vow that I would do anything he asked me to do,

"Whatever you tell me to do, Lord I'll do it. Whatever you ask me to do, Lord, I'll do it."

In that vision I cried out and thanked him for saving me. God reminded me of that night when I cried out to him. Then I knew, I had no choice. I made a promise. Answering the call is not always easy. Especially when you are called to do the very thing that you don't want to do. God called me to go back into the very place that I didn't want to be.

But the LORD said unto me, Say not, I am a child: for thou shalt go to all that I shall send thee, and whatsoever I command thee thou shalt speak. Be not afraid of their faces: for I am with thee to deliver thee, saith the Lord. (Jeremiah 1:7-8 KJV)

The Deployment

So we pulled up in the parking lot and we went around to the back. We walked through and we went into the DART coordinator's office. I passed the yard where I played handball and then I went into the coordinator's office. I went into the dorm and I'm sitting there with fifteen women. Five of them use to rip and run Terrace Ave. with me. I started to share. I looked around and the first thing that came out of my mouth was,

"Jesus is Lord!"

I knew that I wasn't supposed to say it, but that fact is a major part of my story. I can't tell my story without saying that. I went on and finished telling them my story.

The church with the big steps

I knew that God was doing some wonderful things in my life. I had gone through drug counseling, had received training for employment and now I needed to learn all that I could about Him, His will and His ways. I started attending church service on a regular basis. I didn't have a car to drive to church. So I'd go on my bike. I'd start out early so I wouldn't have to rush. My ride from Uniondale would take about thirty minutes. Some days, it would be a good ride and sometimes it wouldn't but I wanted to be there to get a seat at the 11:15 AM service. I worked near the church and afterwards would leave there and go to work.

I would arrive in the parking lot and park my bike by the back entrance. I carried my change of clothes with me and would go in the bathroom and change clothes.

Boldness Meets Humility

There were times when I was hungry at church. I didn't always have the money to buy food. I made just enough to pay my rent. My church had fellowship hour after the 11:15AM service. Church members were asked to bring cakes, soup, crackers, juice etc. to serve while we fellowshipped with one another after the service was over. Most of the time, the after service fellowship meal would be all that I'd have over the weekend. I just didn't have the money to buy groceries all the time. One Sunday, I went down for fellowship and I was so hungry. I looked on the table and there was plenty of everything. I knew I'd be able to eat there, but I really needed a plate for later because I had no food in my refrigerator or cabinets. I stood on the line and I waited and a lady started asking me if I wanted some help.

"Can I help you?"

"I just want a slice of that cake and some cookies."

I wasn't being honest. I wanted more. I needed something for now and for later. I was very hungry.

"Okay, but if you want more, just let me know."

I sat down and ate my food. I tried to eat slowly so I could savor the flavor, hoping that it would last longer. Diana, a member of the church, must've been watching me. After a while, she came over to me with a plate of food wrapped up.

"Take this for later"

"Thank you"

I wanted to cry. I knew only God could do that for me. Only God can answer a prayer immediately. From that day forward, Diana befriended me and became my dear sister in Christ. She looked out for me. She started making sure that I had a ride to church on days that it was too bad for me to ride my bike. She was also a beautician and would do my hair.

Diana and I started hanging out a lot. I even took her to meet my home health client, Mother Clarke. She saw how hard I worked there and she saw the conditions as well. I liked her gentle mannerism and I was always listening to how she spoke to people. She was then and is to this day a very kind, considerate and humble woman. She always carries herself and speaks with humility. That characteristic was foreign to me. I knew that God had her in my life so that I could learn from her. I started by trying to wait before reacting to what people said. I like to tell people I'm delivered not perfect. Sometimes I was successful and

sometimes not.

I use to notice also that people would take advantage of her. So I stepped to her about it.

"Diana, why you let her talk to you like that?"

"I ignore people. Pretty soon, they'll stop."

I looked at her like she had twelve heads. That way of thinking was really foreign to me. Usually I would've just accepted it bur this time, I couldn't. I told her that I wasn't trying to change her in anyway, but I wish that she would consider not letting people take advantage of her. And when they did, call them on it. A couple of days later, she told me that she had taken my advice. She learned some boldness from me and I surely learned some humility from her. There were many other lessons that I learned from Diana. We are still friends and I'm still learning. So is she.

A Passed Torch

*For we are his workmanship,
created in Christ Jesus unto good works,
which God hath before ordained that we should
walk in them.
(Ephesians 2:10KJV).*

New members were asked to come before the session of the church. It was a way for the governing body to get to know you. It gave them an opportunity to find out more about you. We were encouraged to talk about ourselves, our families, occupations and gifts and talents. What may seem unimportant to one person may be a gold mind to another. The Pastor asked me:

"April, what are your hobbies?"

"Hobbies? I don't have no hobbies."

"What do you do?"

"I'm a certified nurse's assistant. I have a patient, a lady in Roosevelt that I work with seven days a week, eight hours a day. I ride my bicycle except when I go to the jail"

"The jail?"

He sat up in his chair.

"What do you do at the jail?"

"I go back there and do an AA and NA meeting. Because my journey is spiritual I tell them about God."

"Tell me more about it."

"If I have extra money, I'll give the sister who doesn't have anything the money"

"Really?"

"Yeah. I don't have a lot but I have more than they have."

"That's good."

After the meeting was over, I left with the other new members. I didn't think any more about the questions he'd asked me or his response. You do what you do and just keep it moving.

A couple of Sundays passed. One day, the pastor asked me to see him after the close of the service. I did. He handed me an envelope with a check in it.

"What is this?"

"Whatever God says. It's for our Prison Ministry."

"What Prison Ministry?"

I didn't know they had one. But I knew that I would love to volunteer.

"The Prison Ministry that you are about to lead."

"Lead?"

"Yes. Lead."

So I gave Diana the check and asked her to be the secretary. That's how it began. Diana and I met at my house and we put together an outline of how we felt the ministry should be run. I knew that whatever it was it had to begin with God first. Putting Him first would make it right. As we sat there, I was starting to understand that everything that happened to me while I was incarcerated happened so that I would see the need to do something about it so that it wouldn't happen to others.

We met with the pastor and he shared that he'd been praying for a leader. There had been a leader eight years ago but she died. I wanted to know why someone else hadn't continued the ministry and I wanted to know what her name was. He told me her name. I immediately thought back to the time when I was incarcerated and she invited me to the church. I believe that God wanted us to meet and connect so that the ministry would be revived. I am forever grateful to Pam for having the fore sight and for visiting me and the other inmates while we were incarcerated.

I started going to church every Sunday. I also started going to Angela Morrison's bible study on Monday and I would go to Gloria Allen's bible study on Spiritual Warfare on Tuesday. I was inspired and encouraged. I really needed the connections that God was building. It was like being with a family. A family that I had just met but one that treated me as though we'd known each other forever. Flaws and all. I was really rough and I know that I needed my edges filed down a bit. God started working on me then and still works with me today on that and anything else that He sees fit to do.

*For I know the thoughts that I think toward you,
saith the Lord, thoughts of peace and not of evil,
to give you an expected end.
(Jeremiah 29:11 NIV).*

Learning to Trust

I had been working with Mother Clarke now for years. I knew deep down inside that I wanted another job but I still felt blessed to have that one, working conditions and all. Another day after the service, the pastor started telling me about this job opportunity. "I'll call you about 10:00AM."

"I don't need a job. I work seven days a week. Eight hours a day."

"I'm setting up an interview for you at Nassau Community College."

"Doing what?"

"Typing. Computer work. Filing."

"I don't know how to do that."

"Trust God, April. Trust God."

I went home and I thought about what he said.

"Trust God, April."

Do I really trust God? I know that I do in other situations. So what makes this one so different? I knew the answer immediately. It's the fear of the unknown. It's the fear of change. I have a problem with change. I also question if I can really do this. Like all things that are important, I started praying for an answer. And the answer came back ever so clear. "Trust God, April."

The next day, I told Mother Clarke's daughter about the job opportunity. She was happy for me but, she was concerned about how it would affect them. She was accustomed to me being there and was very anxious.

"What's gonna happen to us?"

I understood her anxiety. I had been working with her for a while now. I knew them and they were comfortable with me just like I was comfortable with them. But I knew that it was time. "I believe that it's time for me to move on. This would be a job with benefits. A county job. Right now, I don't have benefits. Whatever happens, I pray that you understand."

I knew that I needed to prepare for the interview. I was beginning to trust that it would be alright but, I just didn't think that I had what it took. I had no clerical or computer skills. I called Diana and Gloria and told them about job interview. We decided to meet at Gloria's house that evening to work on a resume. They asked me questions to gather the information.

"What are your skills?"

"I worked as a maid and what I do now. The only other job I had was public servant."

They both knew what type of public servant I meant. We also knew that we wouldn't be able to use it as an employment reference. The next item on the agenda was showing me how to look the part. I really wanted this job so I was open to all they suggested. Wear something blue, black or gray. Modest jewelry.

Don't wear long hanging earrings. And most of all, take out your nose ring. Like I said, I was open to everything they said except that:

"I can't take out my nose ring!"

They looked at me. I think they both realized that it was a closed case. After that, they started asking me interview questions. It really helped me out a lot. I was nervous because, I had never been interviewed before. I was placed in the part time job that I presently have. And the job that I held at the Plainview Hotel, TOPIC House helped me get that one. I felt much better about everything after we were done. With resume in hand, I was ready for my interview.

The next day, Rev. Tuggle picked me up at 10:00AM just like he promised. We drove to the college and went in the Tower building for the interview. The supervisor of the department started asking me questions. The interview questions were very similar to the ones that Gloria and Diana asked me. I was so thankful at that moment that they spent that time with me preparing me for the interview. Just like I expected though, my criminal record came up. I told the truth. I also let them know that I volunteered to go through TOPIC House for two years and that I was presently employed. After the interview was done, I left the room and waited to hear their decision. After a while, I was called back in and told that I was being hired as a part-time employee on contract. I had not taken the civil service exam and would need to take it before becoming a permanent employee of the county. I didn't know what it all meant, but I did know that it would be a new experience for me and I believed that it would make a difference, a positive difference in my life. I was so excited and couldn't wait to get home to call Gloria and Diana and to thank them for helping me reach this milestone in my life.

I was so nervous on my first day of work. There was so much to learn. I was working at the information desk. We were expected to help the students, redirect calls, etc. I tried to write down everything so that I could review it at night. I shadowed some of the other employees but then they wanted me to try answering the phone.

"Hello Nassau County I mean Nassau Community College how can I help you?"

I kept making that same mistake over and over again. I couldn't help it. Because every time that I'd said Nassau in the past the next words were usually County Correctional Facility. After five or six times doing that I excused myself and went over by the copy machine. I could hardly contain myself. I started to cry, "Lord, please bring me through. I'm victorious in Jesus name. You busted this door open for me." Just then a lady from another department came up behind me and she placed her hand on mine. She said, "April, he'll bring you through. Believe it."

I thanked her and returned to my desk. That night when I got home, I cried myself to sleep.

My first weeks were rough. Physical tiredness is one thing but, emotional and mental tiredness is another. I still worked with Mother Clarke because I was part time at the college. I worked with her three days and at Nassau Community College for four days. I rode the bus in one direction to Nassau Community College and I rode my bike in the opposite direction to Mother Clarke's house. I started working in January at the college but didn't get my first check until March.

Through determination and hard work, within a month, I'd learned the campus directory. I could answer the phone and direct calls to any place on campus but I'll be the first to admit that I was a little rough around the edges. I often felt like I was being picked on. The way I talked was scrutinized, the way I answered the phone, everything. I know now that I wasn't being picked on, I was being groomed. Refined. I had to die to some things so that I could be a more efficient employee. One of my coworkers helped me out a lot. He helped me set up an email account and showed me how to use the computer.

"Just take the mouse and move it on the pad"

I looked at the floor and picked up my feet. "We got mice here?"

He looked at me and smiled. He then explained to me what the mouse does and how I could use it to navigate around a document or windows. I felt embarrassed, but his smile spoke volumes. It let me know that no matter what questions I had, I could always come to him and not be embarrassed. It was spiritual and from that moment on, I knew that he would be one of my greatest allies.

A year passed. I knew my job very well. I was now able to train work study students and anyone else that came into the department. I applied for civil service status. A short time later, I received a letter that stated application denied. The application officer called me.

"Is this April Cofield?"

Yes, it is."

"In order for you to complete an application with the civil service we need your criminal record."

"Well here's my Social Security number and you can pull the information."

I knew that I wasn't the first person with a criminal record that had ever applied for civil service status. I felt that I was being tested.

"As long as I'm in this position, you will never be a civil service employee."

"I'm praying for you."

And I did. I prayed for that man every day. I couldn't understand how someone could waste so much energy trying to keep a foot on someone else's neck. I had to renew my contract every six months. In the meantime, the civil service officer kept denying my application. I didn't give up.

One day, a full time position became available. My supervisor wanted me to have it. She knew that I was a diligent worker and she wanted me to be full time. I wanted to be full time. I filled out the civil service paperwork again. I prayed that I would finally get an approval.

July 2004. "April, this is Ted Brynes*"

"I got some good news and bad news. Tell me which one you want first?"

"Give me the bad news first."

"You won't be making the same money that you were making before."

"Whadaya mean I won't be making the same money?"

"Now you are a full time employee and as a-"

Thank you, Jesus! I shouted. I couldn't hear the rest of what he said for a brief moment. I could only praise God for blessing me with my first full time job with benefits. I would start gaining vacation, sick and personal days. I had never had that before.

I kept thanking Him because only He could do this for me. I could trust someone to take care of me and have my back. It was possible. I could trust God.

Many years have passed since April learned to trust God. The prison ministry and its members have grown by leaps and bounds. Their philosophy is simple: meet them where they are and welcome them. April and the other devoted members do exactly that. This ministry calls for special people. It is not a ministry for the weak. You must be spiritually and mentally strong. April exudes strength in both areas. I can bear witness to that! Occasionally, her ministry requires that she goes back to memorable places from her past and help those who are newly released from jail or currently struggling with an addiction. And every week without fail she mentors a group of females who are incarcerated. It is not an easy task but, someone must do it. Someone qualified. Someone called by name. April is qualified and she was called for this task. Besides, she made a promise.

> *Naked and ye clothed me: I was sick, and ye visited me: I was in "PRISON" and ye came unto me.*
> *(Matthew 25: 36 KJV).*

A Promise Kept

God's Great Give Away

The Purpose. When April was incarcerated a group would come every Christmas and give the inmates a plastic green cup filled with candy canes. After returning as a speaker, she found out that they were no longer giving the gifts. Your pain can become your ministry. Who better to connect but you. Such is the case with April. Most of the women that go into the system, only have the clothes on their back. They don't get care packages from home or have money for commissary to purchase items that they need. Only a few inmates are blessed to have family on the outside that care enough to send a care package. The county does not provide extra underwear. So, most women have one or two pairs of underwear. Try being on your period with one pair of underwear. The same thing goes for the socks and undershirts. It's cold inside the facility. They need these items to keep warm. April knows. She spent many nights inside with not enough changes of underwear. She was at the mercy of fellow inmates who knew her and made sure that she had socks, tee shirts and underwear. The Ministry routinely distributes undergarments throughout the year to any woman that requests them.

The Testimony. December 2007. Some of the members from the Prison Ministry met in the parking lot at Nassau County Correctional Facility to unload black garbage bags from their cars. The large heavy bags were filled with brand new, white *cotton underwear, t-shirts and socks. While going through the dorms, I recognized women who I've seen on television. Women, who's cases made the 6:00 news. There were also women whose names I didn't know. Women who will remain nameless. Each of them. Standing in three rows. Patiently waiting their turn to get a pair of sock, a t-shirt and a pair of underwear. A few of the women refused to take the underwear stating that they only wear boxers. They only wanted the undershirt and socks. I looked at them in astonishment. How is it that you can turn down a gift? A gift of personal items that are necessary for your comfort. It wasn't for me to understand. We lugged around extra large black garbage bags with sizes 5-10 underwear, Medium through XXX Large T-shirts, and socks to each dorm. Marsha and I were in charge of underwear. Nancy and Sandy were in charge of t-shirts. Jevota gave out the socks. April handed out food for the soul. A lot of the ladies were in tears and were so thankful for the simple gift. They were truly so thankful. I was moved to tears and I was very thankful to God that I could take part in this evening's ministry.*

It's funny, how even in prison, some of us still have a warped sense of size. I shouldn't have thought otherwise. We don't stop being women because we are incarcerated. Anyway, one lady came up to the table. It was obvious to a duck that she didn't suffer from the missed-meal colic. Bertha (her hips) was pretty pumped up and she needed the largest size underwear we had to cover her up. She came up to the table and proudly asked for a size 6. I was thinking, "She can't be serious!" I opened a pair to show her that the requested size wouldn't fit. They were cotton and would shrink. She didn't care and insisted on taking the 6. I gave them to her. Maybe she will wear them as a scarf to wrap her hair. We all enjoyed a good laugh behind that one!

Birthday for Jesus

The Purpose. Giving gifts at Christmas to the children. Her ministry is based on her inability to provide for the children she loved. As a crack head, she'd buy her children gifts. Then when the money was gone she'd unwrap them and sell them to pay for crack cocaine. Also, when April was sober and an inmate, it always bothered her that she couldn't give her children gifts at Christmas. So, this mission was initiated in honor of them.

The Testimony. Around mid-October, the inmates had given the names and addresses of their children and the caretakers. An invitation was mailed to the families inviting them to a birthday party for Jesus.

December 2007. The Prison Ministry sponsored an annual outreach to give the inmates' children gifts for Christmas. Upon entering the social hall, the mouthwatering aroma of orange chicken, beef and broccoli and other Chinese food entrees meet you at the door and invite you to come in and have a seat. The full course buffet has been donated by Mr. Chen and the members of his church. He is one of the prison ministry members.

The room is bustling with families. There are children of all ages excitedly waiting for the program to begin. Rev. Crayton gave an opening prayer. The program was short and included testimonials from former incarcerated mothers. They thanked the ministry for providing their children with gifts on previous Christmases when they were incarcerated.

This past year, the prison ministry served fifty families, which totaled one hundred fifty children. The items were purchased through private donations, "toys for tots" and a budget provided by the church. They were given gifts of clothing, shoes, coats, and toys. Every child whose name was given to us by an inmate was given gifts. And the children were told that it is from their loved ones on the inside.

If You Tell it, they Will Come!

The Purpose. Your ministry is the Great Commission. The only time that April attended services on a regular basis was when she was incarcerated. The Memorial Presbyterian Church Prison Ministry leads the third Sunday protestant service.

The Testimony. We waited for the inmates to be released from the dorms and escorted to the church on the Inside. The church is small with a single aisle. The wooden pews curve at just the right places so that your back is firmly supported. The fifteen rows are spaced tightly together. The windows on the one wall are screened and barred. The other wall is cement. The altar is bare except for a single cross in the middle. There is an organ and a lectern. There are also the ladies in their green accompanied by a crew of officers. We are all inside and the doors are locked behind them. The service can begin. We start with the first song. Then the second old familiar song: He's Sweet I Know. The women in green sing with their whole hearts and souls. By the second time around, it is evident that their singing is Praise! After completion of the song A lady steps into the aisle and comes to the front. She turns and faces the congregation and begins to pray. Then April speaks.

"Hello my sisters. I greet you in the name of our Lord and savior Jesus Christ. I am your sister April Cofield Essix and we are the Prison Ministry from Memorial Presbyterian Church."

It's all pretty normal. What you'd hear in any church except for what comes out next.

"I use to prostitute on Terrace Ave. Smoke crack as fast as I could cook it up and.... I was known on the street for my mouth." *Someone in the back shouts out.*

"Sho nuff!"

The others laugh. I join them. I know April. I know that what she says is true.

I am there. Sitting. Right side. Second row. Aisle seat. April stands the entire time. She wants to be mindful of the time. Not wanting to go over the service which would inconvenience officers that were on duty until we finished the evening service. She also wants to make sure that the ladies are there for the right reason and not using this time as a social hour. Not on her watch.

"I sat there."

She says.

"In that seat, right there."

Those that know her agree. Those that don't, look at her with skepticism. She notices the look and goes into the lingo that only they understand. They clap for her. Others cheer. She understands them. She has lived their life and knows the pain associated with incarceration. She's outspoken. Raw. She keeps it real. She is their voice. And she is also their hope. Through her testimony they know that they can make it. If a notorious crack head ho can turn her life around then so can they. If she can give her life to Christ then so can they. If her willingness to share her past in her assignment of service to God can be effective enough to change the lives of the forgotten, the least and the lost then they can do the same.

A Prayer Answered

On February 16, 2008, April celebrated thirteen years drug free. The next day, which was Sunday, she celebrated as she always does. She was in church, with her head bowed, standing at the altar and in prayer. This year was different. Attesting to the fact that God does answer prayer, she was joined by her church family, her extended and a few people whose names had been written on numerous prayer cards throughout the year. The most notable person present was her son, Ka'wand.

Her mother was ill that day and couldn't join her, but they presently enjoy a wonderful relationship. Trust has been restored as well as forgiveness. April stated that she never stopped loving her mother. She didn't always like what she did but she always loved her. I'm sure, when asked, her mother will say the same.

April is working at rebuilding the love and trust with her son and daughter. She is still working at healing the relationships with all of her family members. She prayed many years ago that if God saw fit, that He would bring them back to her. Love is patient and love is kind. She believes that He will. In time, she knows that He will.

There is also someone in her life who brings her tremendous joy. The most precious words that you can say to someone is their name. It can bring you tremendous joy when it is said with love. She always wanted to hear the words, "Mommy" And now God has blessed to hear the words, "Grandmommy," by her grandson, Don-tay.

Afterword

I had no idea when I offered her a ride eight years ago what plans God had for the both of us. She promised to tell me a mind-blowing account of her life. I promised to write about it. But I didn't know that when I invited her into my car, I'd welcomed her into my life. She has now become a dear friend to me. She is a dearly loved sister. I've learned a lot from her. I pray that she's learned something from

me.

"Life is a puzzle." That's the metaphor that April uses to describe her journey. There were people who placed pieces next to the ones she placed. There were others who placed pieces with her. And there were those who found misplaced pieces and guided her hand to find the correct space. Her puzzle is not yet completed for there are still

many other pieces to be placed. But for now, chosen for His purpose, this section of the puzzle is completed. And now you understand as I do why she praises with unadulterated thanksgiving! Praising God and thanking Him for what only He was then and is still able to do.

From Crack to Christ: A Witness? (Step aside stones, I got this!) Indeed! Hallelujah! Glory to God! Amen

The "Life Puzzel" That Came Together.

*While reading the Afterword, I realized the puzzle actually has come together, God has done what he said He would do for me . By no means has the puzzle been complete more pieces are being fitted, by the time this is published, I will be approaching 31 years clean and sober, I'm still standing in the gap for the **lost,** the **least** and the **last,** A task only God can see me through, I have been an Ordained Licensed Minister of the Gospel since 2017, I stay in spiritual war fare, thank God for prayer warrior's, thank God for just being God all by Himself. Thank God for the Holy Spirit teaching me what I need to know and reminding me of it through out every day, in Jesus Christ name. I did learn something from Robin. I learned to wait, be still, to speak softly and with authority.*

Thank you, Lord Jesus Christ, For Reverend Reginald Tuggle and Robin Carmon Marshall, thank you for using them for me. **Servant Witness Enduring a Fiery Trial is, Standing Firm No Matter What.**

www.ingramcontent.com/pod-product-compliance
Lightning Source LLC
LaVergne TN
LVHW041705060526
838201LV00043B/592